Stop Struggling, Start Teaching

Stop Struggling, Start Teaching

Katie Van Dyke and Brad Wilcox

CFI
Springville, Utah

ISBN: 1-55517-918-5
e. 1

Published by CFI
an imprint of Cedar Fort, Inc.
925 N. Main, Springville, Utah, 84663
www.cedarfort.com

Distributed by:

Cover design by Nicole Williams
Cover design © 2006 by Lyle Mortimer
Printed in the United States of America

10 9 8 7 6 5 4 3 2 1

Contents

Dedication

To all the Primary, Sunday School, Young Men, Young Women, and seminary teachers who believed in us despite our imperfect behavior, especially Joan Hansen, Judith Nash, Julia Golding, Claud Glazier, Tom LeFevre and, of course, our parents.

Acknowledgments

We would like to thank our families, especially our spouses, Blair and Debbie, for their love and support. Without their assistance and encouragement, this project could not have been completed. Their vision inspired us, and their confidence kept us going.

We acknowledge the expertise of Randall Sprick. His work to improve discipline in the public schools inspired us to bring the same ideas to teachers in the Church. His concepts were a catalyst for this book. J. Lloyd Eldredge, Rodney S. Earle, H. Clifford Clark, and Kristen Goodman also provided us with helpful and practical information.

We express gratitude to all the Primary and Sunday School teachers who were willing to share their experiences and ideas with us, especially Julene Kendall, Caryn Pearce, and Barbara Cromar.

We also express thanks to the staff of Cedar Fort, especially Lyle Mortimer and Lee Nelson for believing the project would fill an important need, Michael Morris and Mindy Higginson for editing the manuscript, and Nikki Williams for designing the cover.

Foreword

When I served as General Young Women President, Brad, who was a professional educator, approached me with concern about what he felt was a lack of resources available for helping lay teachers in the Church handle behavior problems in the classroom in the most positive and effective ways. Brad was working on his master's degree in education at Brigham Young University at the time. He determined that the first step in providing valuable resources for the classroom teacher was to identify what the major problems were. This issue became the focus of his thesis, "Identifying Discipline Problems in LDS Church Classes in the United States: Teacher Perceptions of Student Characteristics, Behaviors, and Backgrounds."

After joining the faculty at BYU, Brad began working with Katie Van Dyke, a graduate student who shares his concern that teachers in the Church be provided with information regarding classroom management. Having identified the major problems that occur in establishing and maintaining positive classroom behavior, Brad and Katie have written a book filled with practical, specific, and useful insights and skills to be used with individuals and groups of various ages. In addition to the skills, techniques, and practices that they identify, Brad and

Katie write from years of their own experience. They are not only focused on the outward behavior of the student, but they are also keenly committed to the sensitivity of each individual, with a reverence for teaching moments that lift the inner spirit of a student to higher levels of performance in conduct and increased motivation for learning.

The importance of this kind of effective gospel teaching is receiving increased emphasis in the Church. Elder Dallin H. Oaks said, "Every member of The Church of Jesus Christ of Latter-day Saints is, or will be, a teacher. Each of us has a vital interest in the content and effectiveness of gospel teaching. We want everyone to have great gospel teachers, and we want those teachers to help all of us find our way back, not just to them but to our Heavenly Father" ("Gospel Teaching," *Ensign*, November 1999, 78).

Similarly, Elder Jeffrey R. Holland maintains, "To teach effectively and to feel you are succeeding is demanding work indeed. But it is worth it. We can receive 'no greater call'" ("A Teacher Come from God,'" *Ensign*, May 1998, 25).

A careful study of this book will help alleviate the stress that can be a part of teaching, add to the enjoyment of students and teachers, and develop a deep feeling of satisfaction in the sacred responsibility of teaching.

—Ardeth G. Kapp

Chapter 1: **Stop Struggling**

Katie's first experience teaching children in a church setting was not as a teacher but as an observer. While visiting out of town, she attended church with a friend. Her friend was a Primary teacher at the time, so Katie attended her class as well as Primary sharing time. As this friend attempted to give her lesson, six little bodies jumped out of their chairs, poked at one another, talked out of turn, and performed other disorderly acts, none of which involved listening to the lesson. At last, the teacher pulled out a flannel board, and for a short while, she was able to engage the children in a story activity. When the class was finally over and they walked down the hall for sharing time, Katie's friend was obviously worn out and frustrated. The only behavioral difference between sharing time and class time was that six entire classes rather than simply six children wiggled in their seats, talked out of turn, and disturbed other children. This all occurred while their tired-looking teachers sat among the children doing little or nothing to resolve the problems.

Since this experience, Katie has served as a Primary teacher, Primary counselor, and Primary president. Brad also has served in Primary, Sunday School, and Young Men, and on occasion as an early-morning seminary teacher. They have learned that the above scenario is not unique.

In fact, in their experience, discipline is one of the most common problems faced by teachers and leaders in the Church. Yet it is also an area where the least amount of information and assistance are provided. Recently, Katie was asked to give an in-service lesson on the topic of classroom control and management. When she asked the teachers to share their discipline strategies with one another, she found that the majority of the teachers had no discipline strategy at all.

We believe that the lack of discipline strategies in LDS classes is due to a lack of understanding of the concept of discipline. Many teachers mistakenly perceive discipline as a strict and stringent means to impose control and order onto others, which is not conducive to love and the influences of the Spirit. This, however, is not necessarily true. Discipline can be the means by which teachers and leaders teach children and young people self-mastery and self-control, thereby helping them to become more receptive to the influences of the Spirit. President David O. McKay said, "I believe that discipline in the classroom, which implies self-discipline and self-control, and which connotes consideration for others, is the most important part of teaching. . . . Disorderly conduct should not be permitted in any class in the Church" ("Guidance of a Human Soul—The Teacher's Greatest Responsibility," *Instructor,* September 1965, 341–42).

Discipline, as referred to by President McKay, does not come about through imposed order and control. Rather, it comes from training and instruction that corrects, molds, and perfects self-control. Self-discipline may lead to more reverent classes, but more importantly, it places children and youth on the pathway toward discipleship. President James E. Faust taught, "The word disciple has the same root as the word discipline. Self-discipline and self-control are consistent and permanent characteristics of the followers of Jesus" ("The Price of Discipleship," *Ensign,* April 1999, 2).

Effective discipline is in accordance with the doctrines of Christ. As we teach the gospel, we are teaching our students what is right. As we teach appropriate behavior through self-discipline, we are helping them understand how to do what is right. Combining both prepares students to choose the right.

In an article in the *Ensign* titled "Helping Children Choose to Behave," Dale F. Pearson shares an experience where he found it helpful to involve students in class discipline. He writes, "Several years ago as a member of a bishopric, I was asked to help a new Primary teacher who was having difficulty with the ten-year-old boys in her class. The boys were restless, inattentive, and occasionally rude and disruptive, and nothing she tried seemed to help."

He attended Primary the following Sunday, and while he was in the room the boys were well behaved. "You are a group of fine young men," he began. "However, your teacher has indicated that from time to time you are inattentive in class. Because I have confidence in you, I feel that together we can find a solution to this problem."

He asked them to help list some of the behaviors they engaged in that might be interfering with others' learning opportunities. The list included such things as moving chairs around, talking, teasing, not raising hands, and other common behaviors. When they finished making the list, Brother Pearson asked what they could do about it. He says:

> At first, the boys were hesitant to speak, but after a full discussion in which they identified some tentative solutions, I gave each boy a pencil and sheet of paper. On the top of their papers they each wrote, "What will I personally do to change my behavior in this classroom?" I stressed the importance of carefully considering their goals. Each one made a list of four or five things he could do. . . . After placing the responsibility

for improvement directly on each boy, we noted considerable improvement in the classroom during the following weeks (*Ensign*, October 1999, 73).

By guiding these boys toward reverence through self-discipline, Brother Pearson was able to move them closer to discipleship. Elder Neal A. Maxwell teaches that "discipleship requires all of us to translate doctrines, covenants, ordinances, and teachings into improved personal behavior. Otherwise we may be doctrinally rich but end up developmentally poor" ("Becoming a Disciple," *Ensign*, June 1996, 14).

A critical element in involving children and youth in the discipline process is love. Terry Warner teaches, "Love makes such a dramatic difference in discipline that we should never think that we can have a lasting influence for good on our children without it" ("I Have a Question," *Ensign*, March 1996, 72). Similarly, in the book *Teaching, No Greater Call*, published by the Church in 1999, we learn, "As we show love to those we teach, they become more receptive to the Spirit. They become more enthusiastic about learning and more open to us and others in the group. Often, they awaken to a renewed sense of their eternal worth and a greater desire for righteousness" (31). Striving to love the students we teach in the way that Christ would love them has a significant impact on the discipline in our classes as well as on their young lives.

Sometimes teachers take on a boss mentality that works against them. They exercise authority over young people, demand accountability, and then, if the students comply and put together a good enough track record, finally the teacher will convey approval and love. That is not how God approaches us as His children. Our caring and love must be constant and unconditional—given first, and given freely through good and bad, transgression or testimony, brilliant success or utter failure. Regardless of their choices, children and youth need our nonjudgmental love.

As they feel genuine Christlike love from their teachers,

students may begin to feel the immense love that Christ has for them. When this happens, they are more likely to develop a sense of their own self-worth and to cultivate a greater desire for righteousness.

Yet the presence of love does not negate the need for discipline. President Spencer W. Kimball taught:

> Jesus lived and taught the virtues of love and kindness and patience. He also taught the virtues of firmness and resolution and persistence and courageous indignation. These two sets of virtues seem to clash with each other . . . , yet both are necessary. If there were but one, love without discipline, love without deep conviction of right and wrong, without courage to fight the wrong, love becomes sentimentalism. Conversely, the virtues of righteous indignation without love can be harsh and cruel. (*The Teachings of Spencer W. Kimball* [Salt Lake City: Bookcraft, 1982], 245)

Firmness, coupled with love, teaches children and young people what is expected of them, while at the same time assuring them they are cared about.

Part of being firm is setting limits. When one fifty-year-old man was called to teach a class of teenagers in Sunday School, he became concerned when the Sunday School president brought him his materials and said, "Good luck. The last two teachers were eaten alive." The man's anxiety increased even more when he received a sympathy card from a friend whom he had told about his new calling.

Despite these reactions, the man showed up on Sunday well prepared. He greeted his class cheerfully, but during the entire lesson the teenagers acted as if he were not even there. They talked about school. They told jokes. And when he tried to settle them down and get their attention, they reacted rudely. He felt totally out of control. After church, he had the following conversation with his wife:

"Those teenagers acted like complete hoodlums." She

listened to him describe the class and then asked, "Did they know where the fences were?"

"What do you mean?"

"It may sound strange," she said, "but I think teenagers are a lot like cows. They'll wander as far as they can and get into all kinds of trouble unless there is a fence. Once they know where the fences are, they are usually content to graze in the center of the field."

The man thought about his wife's comment during the week. He decided to visit all of the class members to learn their names and find out more about them. He even gave each one an assignment for the next class. On Sunday, he went to class prepared with his lesson and prepared to establish fences as well. He greeted the young people as before and then sat down and said firmly, "While I teach you today, I expect you to listen, with no talking. If you have comments, please raise your hand and we'll hear them in turn. But we are learning about the gospel here, and that is important. It is essential that I have your attention."

The man's report to his wife after class was very different from the week before. No, the teenagers were not perfect, and no, they did not sit with their arms folded the entire time, but things had gone much better. He told his wife, "I had to remind them to be quiet several times, and I had to wait and not continue until they were with me, but I made it through my lesson. Two girls even came up after and thanked me." It was a small but crucial victory.

Young children also benefit from limits set with love. Julene Kendall provides the Primary children she teaches with supportive instruction through a program she calls "Reverence Builders." The goal behind this program is to get children to be responsible for their own behavior. She and the children she teaches begin by determining three or four areas that make up a reverent child. In Sister Kendall's class, these areas include listening, talking reverently, and sitting quietly. They begin by working on one area, such as sitting quietly, and when that area is perfected, they start working on another. Each area is represented on a "Reverence Builder" poster, and at the end of class, the children evaluate themselves and put a sticker on each area. They are then given the option of wearing a "Reverence Builder" badge to sharing time and closing exercises. If they choose to wear the badge, they promise to be examples of reverent behavior. One Sunday, a boy in her class decided not to wear the badge, but halfway into sharing time, he decided he wanted to wear it after all. Sister Kendall says that other Primary children will often ask members of her class about their badges. This keeps the children interested, serves as reminder of how they should behave, and helps them feel proud of their own behavior.

President Thomas S. Monson reminds us that if teachers "love their students and have high expectations of them, their self-confidence will grow, their capabilities will develop, and their future will be assured" ("Only a Teacher," *Ensign*, January 1990, 5). As we involve students in discipline, couple love with firmness, and maintain high expectations, we put ourselves in a position where we can stop struggling so much with student behavior and begin focusing more on teaching.

Chapter 2: **Start Teaching**

All teachers in the Church have a unique and precious gift, the gift of the Holy Ghost. As we strive to instill self-discipline in our students, the Spirit will provide us with the inspiration we need for our individual circumstances. Through the power of the Holy Ghost, we can learn to love each of our students individually. We can come to understand their hearts—each with unique needs, anxieties, worries, and concerns. The Holy Ghost will inspire us with specific ways to assist, encourage, calm, and uplift them. Sister Patricia Pinegar, former Primary general president, tells us: "When you feel [the Spirit] while teaching, when you see the students' desire to do good, when you feel peace and love and joy in your classes, please, share these feelings with your students. Please help young people identify the Spirit in their lives. That will be such a powerful blessing for them" ("Tips for New Teachers," *Ensign*, June 1996, 73).

By seeking the Spirit, we will receive insights that will help us create an environment where students can learn and grow. However, just as love must be coupled with firmness, teaching with the Spirit must be coupled with preparation. The Spirit's promptings cannot be an excuse for poor planning on our part.

President Boyd K. Packer writes, "The easiest way to have control over those whom you teach is to teach them something—to feed them. Be well prepared and have an abundance of subject matter organized and ready to serve. There is no substitute for this preparation" (*Teach Ye Diligently* [Salt Lake City: Deseret Book, 1975], 153). Likewise, President David O. McKay said that teaching is the awakening of thought and the convincing of souls of the truthfulness of the message (*Gospel Ideals* [Salt Lake City: Deseret Book, 1976], 191). Our students are less likely to be restless if our lessons awaken their thoughts and convince their souls that what we are teaching is true. To prepare such lessons, we must teach of Christ with variety and purpose.

Everything we teach should point our students toward Christ. We must help others learn of His redeeming powers, His love for us, His example, and His desire for us to return to Him. We must teach of His ordinances, His covenants, and His commandments so that our students will know how to return to Him.

Despite the singular forces of our message, there are a variety of ways to communicate it. Children are naturally curious and respond well to lessons filled with a variety of learning activities. Visuals, stories, object lessons, simple games, songs, and finger plays can make lessons interesting, engaging, and memorable.

It is also important to clarify our purpose while teaching. Some teachers begin lesson preparation by asking, "What should happen in the lives of those I teach as a result of this lesson?" A teacher's goal must not simply be to fill time or cover the material but to fill students and have an impact in their lives. It helps to clarify what those we teach must know, do, and be as a result of the lesson.

Consider the experience of our friend Caryn Pierce as she taught her Sunday School class of seventeen-year-olds and eighteen-year-olds. Sister Pierce had her hands full as she attempted to reach a rather large group of students, who for two years had gone through teacher after teacher because of their poor behavior.

At the beginning of the year, Sister Pierce gave the class a questionnaire asking them what musical groups they listened to, what kind of TV shows they liked, what their talents were, and son on. She says that helped her to know what type of media she was trying to compete with and what interested them. At the end of the questionnaire, she asked them to rate the importance of the Church in their lives and explain what their testimony was based on. She found that every single student who had attention problems in the class rated the importance of the Church as four to six (out of ten) and claimed their testimonies were based on their friends in the ward.

With this in mind, Sister Pierce began preparing her lessons. When she came to the topic of the Atonement, she set a goal to help the students realize the depth of their feelings for Christ. She decided to prepare a lesson that would culminate with individual writing assignments in which she hoped her students would express their deep spiritual thoughts and feelings.

Sister Pierce began the lesson by capturing the students' attention with an object lesson. This led right into a role play where one of the students acted like he was stealing the fast offering money from the clerk's office, was caught, and needed an advocate. This led to a discussion of Doctrine and Covenants 45:3–5, about Christ being our advocate with the Father.

From there, she drew attention to some quotes and scripture references she had fastened to the walls along with pictures of the Savior's crucifixion and His Gethsemane experience. She asked the students to take a few minutes to look up the scriptural references to gain some insight into the Savior's suffering. Then Sister Pierce presented the writing assignment.

She asked, "When have you felt the power of the Atonement in your life?" "What can you do to feel this power more completely?" and "How can you show the Savior your gratitude for His Atonement?" In response to these questions, the students were to write about personal experiences and feelings that completed the sentence "I stand all amazed because . . ." The last part of class was spent sharing what the students had written. Of this portion of the lesson, Sister Pierce says:

> During the writing time, the students listened to some soft music. They were busy at work flipping through their scriptures, writing, pausing, thinking, and then writing some more. I could feel the Spirit so strongly. A few of them would just sit and listen to the music for a few moments as they pondered their thoughts and how to express themselves. A few were glossy-eyed as they listened to a song about the Savior.
>
> The greatest blessing was hearing the wonderful expressions of feelings and experiences. Even the kids who I thought were "on the edge" were so willing to share their feelings. I gained new understanding about these "troublemakers" as they shared their testimonies of the Atonement and how it had influenced their lives. A few of the students shed tears at the realization of the magnitude of the Savior's love and the realization that they were falling short of their responsibilities here on earth.
>
> It was probably the most satisfying class I have ever been involved in as a teacher, and I did not really do much teaching. I prepared the environment, but the Spirit did the teaching. No wonder the students did not want to leave at the end of class.

Sister Pierce was able to help her students because she focused on the Savior and presented material with variety and a clear purpose. She took time to gather quotes, get pictures ready, and choose music for her students to listen to while they wrote. She also planned an object lesson, a role play, and a discussion that involved reading, writing, speaking, and listening. Her preparation went beyond a quick glance at the lesson manual two minutes before the lesson. This excellent preparation paid off as the students became so involved and interested in the lesson that there was little thought of disrupting or misbehaving.

As Sister Pierce continues to fill students and not just time, we are confident that were she to pass another questionnaire to her students, they might rate the Church as more important in their lives and base their testimonies on something more than their friends.

Chapter 3: **Solving Class Problems**

One Sunday, Katie arrived at Church earlier than usual so she could set up her classroom for a special lesson she had prepared. The class that met before hers had not finished, so she stood outside the door to wait. Strange noises came from inside the room. First, there was a bang followed by laughter. Then there was a crash followed by a raised voice. Following that, Katie heard lots of voices talking together, and then more bangs, crashes, and laughter. She wondered what could possibly be going on inside. Finally, after several minutes, there was silence. Moments later the door flew open and out ran a herd of children—perhaps eleven or twelve. When all the children were gone, Katie timidly walked into the room, but she stopped short as she saw cupboard doors flung wide open, chairs overturned in the middle of the floor, trash littered about the room, and an exhausted and clearly frustrated teacher putting his things away. Katie quietly began putting chairs upright and throwing away garbage. The teacher said nothing until his bag was packed; then he turned to her and sighed, "I wish I could whip the lot of them. Or at least call their parents and have them do it." With that, he walked slowly out of the room without even attempting to clean up.

Even though Katie was not inside this class observing the students' behavior, it is easy to surmise that this teacher faced discipline problems that seemed overwhelming. He needed more practical help than someone saying, "Love the children" or "Teach with the Spirit." Our hope is that in the following pages, teachers like this brother can find specific solutions to the most common problems in Latter-day Saint church classes.

We'll offer some general guidelines first, followed by specific instructions in a question-answer format. Obviously, our suggestions do not constitute the only or even the best way to handle all situations. It is impossible to take into account the particulars of every unique circumstance. These suggestions are meant to be starting points—ideas that can be adopted, adapted, or altered to meet the needs of individual teachers and students.

General Guidelines

President Boyd K. Packer writes:

> A successful teacher . . . will start with gentle elements of discipline and move to the more powerful and persuasive types. Actually, they are not more powerful. The more powerful ones are the very gentle ones. . . . The wise teacher does not kill a fly with a sledgehammer or try to adjust a watch with a crowbar. He takes control of the class at the beginning and then keeps that control. It is much easier to maintain control than it is to try to rescue a situation once it has gotten out of hand. . . . Most situations can be controlled with even a slight gesture. If the gesture does not work, the teacher can always apply something a little more intense (*Teach Ye Diligently* [Salt Lake City: Deseret Book, 1975], 132–33).

Begin by working with the students you teach to establish a few simple, clear rules that will help them govern themselves. Explain why rules are important, and discuss what will happen when rules are broken. Post these rules somewhere in class, or use pictures and drawings depicting appropriate behavior for students who are not yet able to read.

Often teachers will give most of their attention to students who are not following the rules by using rebukes or reprimands. Try instead to praise and pay attention to students who are behaving appropriately while ignoring inappropriate behavior. This also includes praising another student, near the misbehaving student, for a desired behavior.

Handle the problem as early as possible. Discipline problems, like fires, are most easily stopped quickly before they are out of control. Use your eyes to discipline. The eyes are one of the most powerful means of communicating. A steady look directed at an offending student is often sufficient to correct misbehavior. Use the power of silence. Many teachers continue to talk over a noisy class. A sudden silence—even stopping midsentence—brings a painful awareness to violators that their actions are not going unnoticed. Do not try to talk over others. Wait or say, "I'm waiting."

If such subtle attempts are ineffective, try something more assertive. Use the power of proximity to discipline. As you continue with your lesson, move closer to disruptive students. This will let them know that you are aware of the misbehavior and that you expect it to stop. If the misbehavior is not corrected by the time you are standing right next to the students, place your hand on their shoulder or head until the misbehavior stops. If this doesn't work, try moving offending students so they are sitting closer to you or away from the attention that may be feeding the misbehavior.

Involve the uninvolved. If you are alert and watch the students carefully, you can often see when the students' interest is lagging or their attention is wandering. Try to involve them at that point. In other words, instead of saying, "Don't talk or fool around," say "Open your scriptures or raise your hand if you agree with what is being said."

Respond to people and against behavior. When certain behaviors are exhibited, be careful not to react against the person exhibiting the behavior; react against the behavior. Explicitly point out that it is the behavior, not the person, that is unacceptable. This will be easier to do when you remember that most children do not act out just to make trouble. Assume a pure motive for misbehavior. Perhaps the children have been sitting for a long time, or they may be tired. If it is fast Sunday, they are probably hungry. Show them that you understand these concerns by saying something like, "I know you have been sitting for a long time, but we only have ten minutes left. I know you can make it." You could also say, "I know it is fast Sunday and you are hungry, but if we work together, we can have a good experience in class today."

Specific Solutions

Attention getting

Q: When I started teaching my Sunday School class, most of the students were fairly well behaved. There was only one boy, Carlos, in my class who was particularly disruptive. I've been working very hard to help Carlos learn to pay attention and behave appropriately, and my efforts seem to be helping. But lately I've been having trouble with a handful of other students who have never before misbehaved. I don't think I have the energy to help all these students pay attention. What can I do?

A: It may be that these students are misbehaving because they want your attention. Most students want and need their teacher's attention because of the important role teachers play in their lives. Because of this, many students figure out ways to get the teacher's attention—even if this means behaving inappropriately. Other students in your class may have noticed all the attention you are giving to Carlos. They may be thinking that if they misbehave they will get similar attention.

Try giving attention to the students who are behaving appropriately. For example, if Carlos is out of his seat making noise, praise the students who are doing what they are supposed to be doing. You could say something like, "I really appreciate those of you who are sitting quietly and listening. You help to bring the Spirit into our class."

It might also be helpful to ignore the inappropriate behavior of a child who is misbehaving. In the case above, for example, you would not want to focus on Carlos by telling him to get back into his seat. In fact, you would not want to say anything to him or even look at him. Simply praise the other students, and then wait quietly and patiently until Carlos sits down. Then proceed with your lesson. As you praise appropriate behavior and ignore misbehavior, the students will learn that you give your attention to those who are doing what is expected of them.

Enlist the help of the other students in your class to ignore inappropriate behavior. President Boyd K. Packer shared an experience where he did all he could do to settle down an "attention-getter." Finally, he turned to the class and disappointedly asked, "Do we have to put up with things like this?" When the boy was faced with the disapproval of his peers, there was a dramatic change in his behavior. President Packer recounts, "Never again was there an outburst in the class, and before long an opportunity arose that gave him a chance to win their approval by well-prepared participation with special personal help" (*Teach Ye Diligently,* 151).

When giving your attention to students who behave appropriately, it may be helpful to remember to praise a variety of students and not always the same ones. Look for the good behavior in each of the students you teach, and praise them for it. This will help ensure that each child receives the attention he or she desires from the teacher.

Remember that you do not have to wait for a misbehavior

to occur before praising the students in your class for behaving appropriately. Whenever the students in class are doing what is expected of them, praise them. Say things like, "Wow! This is such a great class," or "I really like coming to class when you are all acting like this." As you give them your attention in this way, they will learn that you will give them the attention they desire when they make the right choices, and they will also learn what kind of behavior you expect from them.

As often as possible, try to notice when misbehaving students are doing something right. This will help them learn that the most efficient way to get your attention is to behave appropriately.

Talking to others during lessons

Q: Jayla is a girl in my class who consistently talks to those around her during the lesson. When I ask her to stop, she is silent for only a few minutes before she resumes talking. Even after I ask her several times to be quiet, she continues to talk. What can I do?

A: When students talk out of turn, they are often trying to get attention. When you stop what you are doing to ask the child to be quiet, you may actually be feeding the misbehavior. You can help Jayla become a better listener by showing her that you give your attention to those who are behaving appropriately. Start the lesson by stating, "I expect everyone to listen and not talk while I am talking." Then praise the students who are quiet rather than reprimanding Jayla. This will focus the attention on the students who are doing what you want them to do—listening. Be sure to reinforce the "talker" when she begins to listen by praising her appropriate behavior.

If Jayla gets those around her talking so that it is impossible for you to present your lesson, just stop. Don't say anything directly to the students who are talking. Wait until it is completely quiet, and after several seconds of silence, proceed with the lesson. If the students do not respond to your silence, you may need to say calmly yet firmly, "I'm waiting." Then after the students have been silent for several seconds, proceed with the lesson. Remember to praise the students when they are listening to you, even if you just had to stop because of the noise. Again, providing lots of positive feedback will show the students that you focus your attention on appropriate behavior.

It is also important to remember that students need to participate in class. Teacher presentations should be balanced and allow time for student involvement. You may find that Jayla will be more willing to listen when you provide plenty of opportunities for her to be actively involved in the lesson. For example, at some point during the lesson, say to the class, "Discuss this point with the person sitting next to you." After using this technique a few times, simply call out "Share!" and let the students turn to their neighbors and start talking. Follow up with a general discussion that will probably be richer because the students have already talked about the topic in pairs. For younger students, a stuffed teddy bear can be used to gain the students' attention. During the lesson, the bear "watches" for students who are participating, and at the end of the lesson or activity, the bear gives them all a kiss.

Talking loudly or shouting at the beginning of class

Q: My class tends to be very noisy before the prayer is said. They shout and talk loudly and generally act rambunctious. I have to shout over the top of the noise to get them ready to say a prayer, and while they generally quiet down for the prayer, immediately afterwards the noise level rises once again. What can I do to help them come into class reverently and remain reverent?

A: It might help you to know that students do not usually act rambunctious out of spite or malice. They do it because it is fun and possibly because it makes them feel free and full of energy. The students in your class may not even realize they are acting so irreverently, so you might want to discuss the problem together. When they understand that their behavior is a problem, they may possibly be willing to help come up with some solutions to this problem.

To begin with, you might want to discuss with the students how they think they should behave as they come into class. Tell them that you expect them to come into class ready to learn. Let them know that it is fine for them to talk to one another as long as they talk reverently and quietly. You could have reverent music playing as they come into class to remind them of things you discuss. You could also write questions relating to the lesson on the board and ask them to read them and think about them as the other students are coming in. You could even hand them paper and pencil and have them write a response to the questions.

Something else you might try is to develop a signal you can give if the class becomes too loud. This signal, which could be turning off the lights or snapping your fingers, should remind the students that they need to talk more quietly. Whatever signal you decide on, remember to give it initially without saying anything. Simply wait patiently until the class quiets down. After a time, if the class members do not become reverent, you could move closer to those who are being disruptive or say firmly, "I'm waiting." You might even want to have the students practice responding to the signal. Allow them to begin talking to one another, give the signal, and then time them to see how long it takes them to settle down. Praise them for their efforts and tell them how much you appreciate their reverence. This signal may be effective at other times during your lesson as well as at the beginning of class.

Finally, to ensure that the class remains reverent between the opening prayer and the beginning of the lesson, keep in mind that effective lessons begin by capturing the learners' attention. One way to do this is to use an object lesson to begin your teaching. Object lessons relate intangible principles to familiar objects. Charles Hobbs explains how the Savior frequently used object lessons:

Jesus Christ chose the object lesson as one of his most popular methods of instruction. . . . He pointed out that the eyes are the light of the body. Pointing to the lilies of the field and the fowls of the air, he taught that God provides. Quite possibly Jesus held a mustard seed in his fingers and observed a mountain while teaching the principle of faith . . . the city gate became the way of eternal life; bread and water, his body and blood; an oxen yoke, the easy burden of the gospel. . . . The lost sheep became a lost soul. Fishermen became fishers of men. By example our Lord consistently taught the importance of teaching with objects. (*Teaching with New Techniques* [Salt Lake City: Deseret Book, 1965], 107–8)

Telling stories is another way to get the attention of the students in your class at the beginning of a lesson. Stories can help learners apply the gospel principles as they share in scriptural events, moments of decision, hardships and struggles, and the blessings of living the gospel. Stories make gospel principles easier to understand and remember, and they show how gospel principles can be applied to our lives. Just as the Savior used object lessons in His teaching, He also used stories. His parables are excellent examples of using stories to teach (see *Teaching, No Greater Call* [Salt Lake City: The Church of Jesus Christ of Latter-day Saints, 1999], 179).

Other attention-getting activities might include flannel boards, overheads, music, drawing activities, or simply rearranging the seating so that the students are not facing the usual direction. You might even try beginning with a challenging question or idea that stimulates thinking. Younger children respond to finger plays and activity verses. Even if young children do not participate in the finger plays, they still enjoy watching, and their attention is captured in this way. The *Friend* magazine publishes activities for young children, and the *Primary 1* manual contains fun finger plays. Some examples include:

"A Place for You" (3)

If you're very, very tall (stretch and reach arms up),
There's a place at church for you. If you're very, very
small (crouch down), There's a place at church for
you.

Tall (stretch up) Small (crouch down) Tall (stretch up)
Small (crouch down) Heavenly Father loves us all.

"God's Creation" (9)

God made the moon (make a circle with hands)
And winking stars (open and close hands)
And put them in the sky (reach up).
He made the sun (make a circle with arms overhead)
And trees (hold arms straight up)
And flowers (cup hands)
And little birds that fly (wave arms).

"I'm Glad I Came to Church Today" (138)

I'm glad I came to church today (clasp hands, make
steeple by putting forefingers together)
I love to listen (cup hand around ear)
And to pray (fold arms and bow head).
I learn of Jesus up above (point up).
I think of Jesus and His love (hug self).

Talking or acting irreverently during prayer

Q: My students seem to have trouble maintaining reverence during the prayer. At worst, they talk, whisper, or giggle to one another. At best, they sit quietly, but their arms aren't folded and their eyes aren't shut. How can I help my students behave more appropriately during the prayer?

A: Reverence during prayer is important because it sets the tone for the class and helps children and young people prepare to learn the gospel. Discuss this principle with your students so that they will understand the importance of reverence during prayers. During your discussion, you will probably want to talk with your class about appropriate ways to behave during prayers. It might be a good idea to invite their responses. Some of these responses might include sitting quietly, folding arms, bowing heads, closing eyes, keeping feet quiet, and so forth. You could try writing these responses on a prayer chart, and when it is time for prayer, you could hold up the chart to remind your students how to behave during prayer. For younger children who cannot read, you could use a picture of a child who is ready for prayer. Do not begin the prayer until everyone is ready.

If students begin talking or whispering during the prayer, move closer to them and touch them lightly on the shoulder. Keep your hand there until they behave appropriately. By doing this, you should be able to solve the problem quietly without disrupting the prayer. Be sure to thank those who were reverent during the prayer by saying something like, "I appreciate all of you who were reverent during the prayer. You've helped us get ready to learn by inviting the Spirit into our class. Thank you."

If the behavior of one or two students still does not improve after you have tried the above for several weeks, you will probably have to talk with these students privately. During your private discussion, you could ask, "What is the problem here?" Answering this question will help them identify their own inappropriate behavior. You could then ask, "Is that helping us?" Disruptive students can then make a value judgement of their own. Have the students come up with a plan of their own by asking, "What can you do about it?" Then say something like, "Will you shake on it?" to get students to commit to their plan. Before a prayer, discreetly remind students of the plan and the commitment. When the students make it through a prayer without being disruptive, be sure to offer plenty of praise and encouragement.

Laughing and giggling

Q: I have a boy in my early-morning seminary class named Colin who has a really good sense of humor.

We were having a discussion the other day in class, and all the students were participating. Colin raised his hand, and I called on him to contribute to the discussion. The comment that he made enhanced the lesson, yet it was very funny at the same time. Everyone was laughing, including me. It was a truly joy-filled moment. Since then, however, the students are constantly trying to make one another laugh, and instead of bringing joy into our class, the laughing and giggling have become disruptive, occurring even during prayer. How can I control the giggling and still allow for some spontaneity in my class.

A: Perhaps the reason the students in your class are trying to make one another laugh is because of the joy they felt when everyone was laughing together. They want to repeat that situation, and they probably want the attention that Colin received when it happened. To help control the giggling, you may want to discuss the problem with your class. You could begin by asking them why they are trying so hard to make the other students in the class laugh. Accept their responses, and continue by telling them that the laughter has become a problem. Ask them to come up with some reasons why they think it might be a problem. Once the problem is understood, ask them to share their ideas about when laughing is appropriate and when it becomes disruptive. From this discussion, come up with some clear expectations regarding laughing during the lesson. You might even think about making these expectations part of your class rules.

Once the students understand the problem and know what is expected of them, you can help the students live up to these expectations by ignoring those who continue to laugh and praising the students who are cooperating with you. As you praise the students who are not laughing, you are demonstrating that you give your attention to students who behave appropriately.

It is also important, however, to help students understand

that joy-filled laughter is not only acceptable but also desirable in the class. When this type of laughter occurs in your class, laugh with the students and enjoy doing so. President Boyd K. Packer wrote, "Practice looking for the humorous side in teaching situations. . . . You might be surprised at the change it can make in the attitudes of those whom you teach, the ice it can help break, the warm feelings of joy it can generate" (*Teach Ye Diligently*, 215). (For more about humor in the class, see "Joking and making smart-aleck remarks," page 30.)

Having chaotic discussions—talking about the lesson but out of control

Q: When I first began teaching my class, we had productive discussions where everyone participated and cooperated. But lately our discussions have turned chaotic. The students are interrupting one another; they are talking loudly just to be heard, and all my energy is spent trying to be a mediator. I'm beginning to think I should teach the lesson by lecturing without asking for any input from the students. What do you think?

A: Meaningful discussions are fundamental to gospel teaching. Discussions can bring results that seldom occur without them. These results include promoting diligent learning, encouraging unity among those you teach, increasing understanding, and reducing misunderstanding (*Teaching, No Greater Call*, 63). When you have discussions with the students in your class, you show them that you care about what they think and that their ideas matter. Even though their participation seems chaotic, their eagerness to participate in the discussions shows that they are excited about being able to share their knowledge and opinions. To make your discussions more productive, it could be helpful to establish a few simple ground rules. First, you will probably need to decide if your class is mature enough to have discussions without raising their hands. If they are, your ground rules for discussions might include some of the following:

1. Listen attentively to others while they are talking.
2. Wait for your turn to talk.
3. When it is your turn to talk, talk in a tone that would invite the Spirit into class.

If you feel like the students you teach need to raise their hands in order to have a successful discussion, your second rule might read, "Raise your hand and wait until you are called on to talk." You might even find it helpful to allow the students to help you come up with these rules.

Once you have established some ground rules for your discussions, think about writing them out and posting them somewhere in your class to remind the students of what has been decided. Praising the students who follow the rules will also help the other students remember how to participate in discussions appropriately. Likewise, ignoring the students who do not follow the rules will show the students that you give your attention to appropriate behavior.

You may also find it effective to vary the types of discussions your class has. The following ideas may be helpful:

1. Case Study: A case study is an open-ended story. When the story reaches its climax, the teacher says, "What would you do?" The students then seek to find solutions to the problem through class discussion. At the end of the discussion, a summary is made, and the students conclude what action they plan to take when encountering similar problems.
2. Panel Discussion: Two to six participants stand in front of the group while the teacher directs and controls the discussion. The teacher presents a problem, and panel members present their views concerning the problem. The teacher and other class members ask questions and make comments to which the panel members can respond. Panel members respond informally to these questions. The teacher

steers the discussion toward the chosen topic, ties up loose ends, and summarizes the ideas that have been presented.

3. Question Box: Begin by giving the students a small slip of paper to write down anything they would like discussed with the group. Each paper can be anonymous. The teacher then puts the slips of paper in a box, draws one out, and reads it silently (This ensures that no inappropriate questions are presented before reading aloud). The students then discuss solutions to the problem, and the teacher helps to summarize the ideas that are presented (*Teaching with New Techniques*, 177–80).

Calling out answers without raising hands

Q: In my class, the students and I have established specific rules that are posted each week. One of the rules is to raise your hand when you have something to say. The students generally adhere to this rule, especially during discussions and when they want to make a comment, but when I ask a question, it seems that they are all so eager to answer that they forget to raise their hands. Is there anything I can do to help the students remember to raise their hands when answering questions?

A: You are probably right that the students are calling out answers in order to be the one to answer the questions. The students are excited about what they know and want the chance to demonstrate that knowledge. To remedy the problem of calling out answers, it might be helpful to look at your own reaction in these situations. Often, without realizing it, teachers accept called-out answers and move on without giving the students with their hands raised a chance to respond. Students learn quickly that the best way to be acknowledged by the teacher is to call out the answers instead of raising their hand.

Try ignoring the called-out answer, even if it is the correct one, and ask a student with a hand raised to respond. When that student answers the question, you could say something like, "Thank you for that wonderful insight. I especially liked the way you remembered to raise your hand." This can teach students that the best way to be acknowledged by the teacher is to raise their hands. You could also remind the students that you expect them to raise their hands by phrasing your questions this way, "Raise your hand if you can tell me why Joseph Smith had to wait four years to receive the gold plates?" Calling out answers has probably become a habit for some of the students, so a gentle reminder like this will make it easier for them to remember to raise their hand when they want to answer a question.

Your class may also learn to raise their hands when you make an effort to give everyone a chance to respond. If you direct follow-up questions to those who were not chosen to answer the original question, the students in your class will learn that they will get a chance to participate. Another idea that gives everyone a chance to participate is to write questions on word strips and tape the word strips to the bottoms of chairs. At appropriate times during the discussion, ask students to remove the question from their chair. Then have them read the question and respond to it (*Teaching, No Greater Call,* 70).

Joking and making smart-aleck remarks

Q: I have several students in my class who joke around or make smart-aleck remarks when they answer questions or make comments. These remarks always produce a ripple of giggles among the other students in class. These giggles are almost as disruptive to the lesson as the jokes and smart-aleck remarks that caused them. What can I do to stop the joking and smart-aleck remarks as well as the giggles that come with them?

A: You could begin to resolve this problem by discussing the problem with the students. Ask them why they feel like they have to make smart-aleck remarks. Once they have explained, you could ask them to come up with reasons why those remarks are not appropriate in class. Their responses may include, "They could hurt the feelings of others," "They could be sacrilegious," or "They may distract from the spirit in our class." When the students understand that the remarks are disruptive, they may be willing to stop making them.

Following the discussion, you might want to create a class rule regarding the principles you talked about. This new rule may sound something like this: Comments and answers to questions should invite the Spirit into our class. When this rule is in place, ask each student to verbally commit to follow it. At the beginning of the next class or before you ask another question, remind the students of their commitment. Then praise the students who follow the rule and ignore any further smart-aleck remarks. Also praise students who ignore the smart-aleck remarks. When you do this, these students will learn that smart-aleck remarks diminish when they do not receive the anticipated response. You will also be giving your attention to those students who are behaving appropriately. As you work to decrease the smart-aleck remarks, keep in mind that there is a place for humor in the class. We all enjoy laughter. Some of the most effective lessons and presentations incorporate humor to capture attention or highlight important points. The students in your class want to laugh, and they want you to laugh with them. Charles Hobbs has said, "A teacher with spontaneous humor and enthusiasm can raise a class of twenty average students to unlimited heights as doers and teachers of truth" (*Teaching with New Techniques,* 25). As you prepare your lessons, you may want to prayerfully consider ways that you can include the power of humor in your lessons. (For more about humor in the class, see "Laughing and giggling," page 25.)

Arguing with others

Q: Lately, my class seems to be arguing all the time. They argue about where they are sitting; they argue about whose turn it is to say the prayer; they argue about who is, or is not, being reverent; and they argue during discussions. It's hard to invite the Spirit into such a contentious class. How can I help the students learn to interact positively with one another?

A: The first thing that might help is to eliminate the sources of some of the arguments. For example, if the students argue about where they are sitting, give them a fixed seating arrangement. If they argue about whose turn it is to say the prayer, create a prayer chart. By letting the students know in advance where to sit and whose turn it is to pray, you will eliminate some of their reasons for arguing.

The next thing to consider is why your class is arguing so much to begin with. Most likely, they are arguing for one of two reasons. First, they may see arguing as a way to get attention. When you step in to stop arguments or to help settle disputes, this attention may be reinforcing their negative interactions. If you feel this might be the case, refer to "Attention getting," page 18.

Another possible reason is that your class may simply not realize how much they are arguing with one another. Under these circumstances, you may be able to help your class by first calling attention to the behavior in a creative way and then motivating the class member to change it. Randall Sprick shares this idea in *The Solution Book: Managing Classroom Behavior* (Chicago, Ill.: McGraw-Hill, 2001). Begin by dividing the chalkboard in half. Put a smiley face at the top of one half and a frowny face at the top of the other. As the students interact with each other, put a check mark under the smiley face if the interaction is positive or under the frowny face if it is negative. When the students ask you what you are doing, explain to them that you will tell them at the end of class.

At the end of class, ask the students if any of them figured out what you were doing on the chalkboard. After they have learned that you were keeping track of their positive and negative interactions, help them understand why you are concerned about all the arguing. Allow them to offer their own ideas about why their arguing needs to stop. Then include these ideas in your class rules. For example, perhaps you discussed the ideas that the Spirit cannot dwell where there is so much contention and that everyone's comments need to be respected. From these ideas, your class rule could be something like, "We will invite the Spirit into our class by eliminating contention and respecting the comments of others." It will probably be beneficial to let your class help you come up with whatever rule you decide on.

With the rule in place, begin praising the students when they interact positively. If, however, they begin to argue, stop what you are doing. Do not say anything. Show them by looking at them that you are disappointed and that you expect the arguing to stop. When the arguing has stopped, move on with your lesson. At the end of class, discuss with the students how they did. You could give them examples of positive interactions you noticed and praise them for their efforts. You may also wish to discuss a few of the negative interactions and ask the students what they might have done differently. Finally, encourage them to keep trying.

Making annoying noises

Q: I have a few students in my class who are constantly making annoying noises. They rap on their chairs; they pat their cheeks with their hands; they make popping sounds with their lips or clicking sounds with their tongues. The noises are exasperating, and when I ask them to stop, they simply look at one another and giggle. How can I help these students stop making these annoying sounds?

A: These students are most likely making these sounds to get your attention or the attention of the other students. Remember that even negative attention can be reinforcing for students, so when you reprimand them and show your exasperation, you may actually be encouraging them to continue their inappropriate behavior. To help these students stop making annoying noises, you could start by following the suggestions found in "Attention getting," on page 18.

It is possible that these students are not making annoying noises to get attention but because they are simply restless. Remember that it is difficult for students to sit still for long periods of time, and they may need help to listen and participate actively. You might consider taking a break to sing a wiggle song. Try "Do As I'm Doing," 276; "Head, Shoulders, Knees, and Toes," 275; "Hinges," 277; or "I Wiggle," 271 (*Children's Songbook* [Salt Lake City: The Church of Jesus Christ of Latter-day Saints, 1989), or do some stretching activities. Once you have done this, you could say encouragingly to your class, "Now that we've got our wiggles out, I know we can make it through the rest of the lesson with no extra noises." Something else to consider is to make sure you include a variety of different teaching methods in your lessons. Incorporating teaching methods such as music, drawing, movement, and other similar activities into your lesson will give your students opportunities to become actively engaged in learning.

Finally, it is important to discuss reverence with the students you teach. Help them understand that reverent behavior is pleasing to Heavenly Father and that as they are reverent, they will feel good inside and their testimonies will grow (*Teaching, No Greater Call*, 83).

Using poor listening skills

Q: The students in my class are not disruptive. In fact, during most of the lesson, they are calm and quiet. Yet I worry that they are not listening. I always have to repeat questions before they can answer them, and they seldom participate in discussions. How can I help them become better listeners and, ultimately, better learners?

A: One of the most effective ways to encourage students to become better listeners is to give them reasons to listen. In school, students need to listen to do well on tests, complete assignments, and receive good grades. In church classes, students do not have such motivations, but they still need reasons to listen. You might find it helpful to discuss these reasons with your class. During your discussion, you could bring out ideas such as (1) listening is one way to show respect and love for others; (2) by listening attentively, we are following the example of the Savior; and (3) listening helps us learn important gospel principles so that we can make correct choices.

Once the students you teach understand the importance of listening, you could encourage them to listen to one another by following these suggestions found on page 67 of *Teaching, No Greater Call:*

1. After one person has responded to a question or offered an insight, invite the others to either add to the comment or express a different opinion.
2. When someone asks a question, redirect it to others rather than answer it yourself. For example, you could ask, "Would anyone care to answer that question?"
3. In advance, ask one or more people to prepare to summarize the ideas that are shared during a discussion.
4. Before a story or scripture you could say, "Listen for the three reasons that Barbara decided to choose the right," or "Listen for the main reason that Nephi built a ship."

To encourage younger students to listen, you may need to simplify these ideas. For example, you could provide them with color cards. Green cards signal "I agree." Red signals "I disagree." And yellow signals "I'm not sure." When questions are asked or comments are made, you could ask the students to signal their answer with one of their color cards. Students could also signal a thumbs-up or thumbs-down.

Finally, do not underestimate how important it is for you to be a good example of listening. *Teaching, No Greater Call* directs teachers, "Make every effort to listen sincerely to learners' comments. Your example will encourage them to listen carefully to one another. . . . As you listen carefully to those you teach, you can help meet their needs for Gospel learning" (64–65).

Not following directions

Q: The biggest problem in my class happens when we transition from a teaching situation into another activity such as a game or art project. After I give directions, more than half of the students ask, "Now what are we supposed to be doing?" or simply proclaim, "I don't get it." How can I help them to follow directions more efficiently?

A: To begin with, make sure you have the students' attention before giving directions. You could provide the students with a signal such as ringing a bell or turning off the lights. You could also say, "I need to give you directions for a new activity. I'll wait until I see everyone's eyes on me."

Once you have the students' attention, demonstrate the task that they are to do while giving verbal directions at the same time. When you are done with the demonstration, go through the directions once more, this time providing the directions in writing as well as verbally. Post the directions somewhere in your class so your students can refer to the list of instructions instead of asking for you to repeat them.

Finally, have the students in your class repeat the directions before starting. Remember to keep the directions clear and concise, and limit the number of directions you give at one time. You can do this by outlining the steps of the task beforehand, then you could practice following the directions yourself to make sure they are adequate. Be sure to not pass any materials to distract students until directions are clearly understood.

Being disrespectful

Q: I have just been called to teach a class that is known for being very difficult. Teacher after teacher unsuccessfully attempts to teach them, yet they are disrespectful in every way: they don't listen, they talk back, they make jokes, they tease, they shout—the list could go on and on. Is there any way that I can earn their respect and have an impact for good on their lives?

A: In answer to this question, consider a story found in the *Ensign* titled "A Class Labeled Impossible." In this story, April Ross tells how the teacher of their impossible class was able to earn their respect and impact their lives for good. She begins the story by explaining that the teacher asked them to introduce themselves.

A few giggles escaped here and there as some called out false names. He seemed to accept them without a clue about the deception. I felt sorry for him. With a patient smile that we would all come to know quite well, Brother Charington asked a question of a girl sitting next to me. To our surprise, he used her real name, not the false one she had given. That was the first of many instances that led us to expect the unexpected from our new teacher.

The next Sunday, we were ready for him again. All the chairs had been moved into a far corner. When the teacher walked into the room, we were all staring at the floor. Our scheme was to sit huddled in the corner and not look up. Brother Charington greeted us cheerfully. Then we heard the rustling of a paper sack and a few other noises we couldn't discern. I did the unforgivable and peeked, and so did others. Brother Charington was arranging scrolls and brass-looking plates on the table. With a calm voice, he began talking about the Book of Mormon. He asked us questions from time to time, and before we knew it we had all moved near him.

By using principles of love and showing interest in us as individuals, Brother Charington taught us in spite of ourselves. (March 1999, 42)

Brother Charington was successful in teaching this disrespectful class because he followed a few simple principles. First, he did not give attention to their disrespectful behavior. He ignored their attempts at calling out false names and surprised them by knowing their real names. He also ignored them when they were all huddled in one corner. Instead of calling attention to their disrespectful behavior, he focused on the interesting lesson he had prepared, and soon the students focused on it as well.

The second effective principle Brother Charington followed was that of having patience. He apparently understood that it takes time to influence the behavior of others, and he exercised this patience with this class. This is evidenced by the students coming to know his patient smile so well.

Probably the most effective principle Brother Charington followed was that of being prepared. He was prepared with attention getters to peak the interest of the class, such as bringing in the scrolls and brass plates, and he presented exciting lessons that the class found more interesting than their tricks and pranks. Taking the time to create prayerfully prepared lessons can be one of the most effective ways to combat discipline problems in the class.

Finally, Brother Charington took the time to show love and interest in his class members. Before he had even met them, he took the time to find out the students' names. And later in the story, the author describes an essential lesson he taught her by knowing that she could not swim. If we want students to pay attention during class, we should try paying attention to them outside of class. If respect is what a teacher wants, respect is what that teacher must be prepared to give.

Making light of sacred things

Q: The students in my class often treat serious subjects as trivial and unimportant. I feel like this is showing disrespect for important gospel topics. Is there anything I can do to change their attitudes about subjects that I feel are sacred?

A: The answer to this question can be found in the following experience of a teacher whose class members were demeaning the things she held dear. This teacher was teaching a group of ten to eleven-year-old girls when they were discussing the mission and martyrdom of the Prophet Joseph Smith. The girls became silly and disrespectful. The teacher listened with disbelief to the irreverent comments and then took a moment to decide what to do. Then, with emotion in her voice, she announced firmly that their talk and laughter were inappropriate and that their words offended the deep reverence she felt for Joseph Smith and his experiences. The girls immediately became quiet. The teacher told them that she loved them and that she enjoyed teaching their class, but that she could not allow such behavior to continue. It was a sobering experience for the teacher as well as for the members of her class (*Teaching, No Greater Call*, 83).

Show the students in your class that you hold gospel truths close to your heart by not allowing those truths to be belittled. Bear your testimony to them of the things you hold most dear. Teach them that light-mindedness is a deliberate irreverence that trivializes the sacred and can become sacrilege and blasphemy. Perhaps light-mindedness regarding sacred things is the "excess of laughter" and "light speeches" about which scripture warns us (see D&C 88:69, 121; 59:15). Clearly, Church doctrines are not to be objects of humor. We must "trifle not with sacred things" (D&C 6:12).

Teasing others

Q: I am concerned about the mean comments and name-calling that are going on among the members' of my class. It seems that the longer it goes on, the more frequently it occurs. What can I do to stop the teasing and negative talk in my class?

A: It might be helpful to consider that most people who tease or bully others are simply demonstrating that they don't feel good about themselves. They are usually feeling unloved or powerless to change certain undesirable aspects of their own lives. Still, such understanding does not excuse the misbehavior. Teasing should not be tolerated in any class. The class should be a place where students feel safe and secure. It should be a place where they can develop positive feelings of self-worth, yet this cannot happen if they are being teased or if other students are being mean. Discuss these ideas with the members of your class. Help them to see how inappropriate teasing is in any situation, and then have them commit to stop teasing and being mean to one another.

Sister Alice Workman shared an experience of how she was able to get her children to commit to stop teasing one another at home. Her suggestion would be equally effective in a class setting. Sister Workman had been wondering how she could stop the name-calling in her home when her oldest son mentioned that his Primary lesson had been about the people of Anti-Nephi-Lehi. She remembered that this was the story about the Lamanites who had been converted by the Spirit through the teachings of Ammon and his brothers. They had repented and buried their weapons of war, covenanting with God that they would never use them again (Alma 24:15–19). Sister Workman thought that if the people of Anti-Nephi-Lehi could bury their weapons or swords, then her family could bury their weapons—their words.

The following family home evening took shape. First, she asked her oldest son to tell the story of the people of Anti-

Nephi-Lehi. Next, she prepared some small slips of paper on which to write the words and phrases that needed to be buried. As a visual aid, she used the Mormonad poster showing a boy with knives flying out of his mouth with the caption "Cutting remarks are really hurting." She then had the children write down on the little strips of paper the objectionable words and phrases they had been using. They had a ceremony of burying their "word weapons," and they promised not to use them again. Sister Workman's family leaves the Mormonad poster hanging in a prominent place as a reminder to speak kindly to one another, and when someone forgets and uses unkind words, he or she is reminded that those words have been buried ("Cutting Out Cutting Remarks," *Ensign*, September 1999, 73).

Like Sister Workman's family, your class could discuss the story of the Anti-Nephi-Lehies and bury their "word weapons" as a way of committing to stop teasing others. You could also use the Mormonad poster or something similar as a reminder to the members of your class that they have committed to stop teasing each other.

Forming cliques that leave others out

Q: I have a few members of my early-morning seminary class who do not seem to be included by the other students. These other students are good friends, and they hang out together at school, so I'm not sure they are willing to accept anyone else into their group. I'm worried about the excluded students' feelings. In class they act withdrawn and unsure of themselves. Is there anything I can do to bring unity into my class?

A: In answer to your question, consider the experience President Boyd K. Packer had when he asked a student body president and a high school prom queen to help him with a girl whom he described as helpless and almost hopeless:

One day I called the two of them into my office and

asked if they would like to perform a miracle. They were interested. I told them some miracles were a little slow in developing, but they were miracles nevertheless. We then talked a little about the girl, and I made assignments. The student body president was to smile and speak to her every time he saw her around school. That was all. He didn't have to take her on a date; he didn't have to stop and talk to her; he didn't have to associate beyond that or single her out—merely the happy, encouraging "I think you're great" or "Hello, how are you today?"

The queen accepted the assignment of walking with the girl across the road from the high school to the seminary. That was all. She didn't have to include her in her circle of friends other than to walk to and from the seminary every day. . . .

The two of them went about their tasks quietly and enthusiastically, saying not a word to anyone else. The miracle was not long in coming. One day I knew there was something different about the girl. It took me most of the class period to figure out what it was. And then I saw what it was. She had combed her hair that day. That was an event!

Over the next two months, the transformation continued. . . . Our wallflower transformed herself, went to college, found good employment, married in the temple, and those who know her would never believe the ugly duckling of her youth. (*Teach Ye Diligently*, 149–50)

You could have the same lasting effect on your students by following President Packer's example. First, be like President Packer and have faith in your students. Have faith that your excluded students can flourish, and have faith that your other students will help. With the help of the Spirit, you can come up with a plan that will fit the needs of everyone in your class. Second, be patient. The miracle may not happen overnight, but with the help of the Spirit, it can happen, and you will bring unity to those you teach because, as Joseph Fielding

McConkie has said, "The Spirit that comes of the Lord is positive, not negative; it brings unity and faith" (*Teach and Reach* [Salt Lake City: Bookcraft, 1975], 20).

Skipping or missing class while at church

Q: I have a student named Angelique who comes to church but fails to attend my class. I have called her on the telephone and personally invited her to join our class. Additionally, other class members have extended invitations to Angelique to become a more active member of our class. Still she continues to skip class. I feel that I have made every reasonable effort to remedy this situation. Are there additional suggestions that you could recommend?

A: You are right to be concerned about Angelique. When you were called to serve as a teacher you were also given the responsibility of maintaining a safe environment for all the students under your care and supervision. Angelique's parents have "released" her to you during your class time, and the underlying assumption is that you will be responsible for her safety during that block of time. Since she is not attending class, you should contact her parents and let them know that Angelique is somewhere other than her assigned class. The tone and tenor of this teacher-parent communication will be most profitable if it reflects a sense of concern and love for their daughter. Additionally, it would be helpful to notify the auxiliary leaders or presidents who share an interest in Angelique's welfare.

Once parents and church leaders have been properly notified of the problem, the teacher could then wholeheartedly focus on shepherding Angelique back to the flock. This usually requires personal contact and singular expressions of love and concern. Ezekiel 34 holds several keys to successful shepherding. In this chapter the Lord reproves mortal shepherds (leaders and teachers) who care more for their own interests than they do for their sheep (students). Following the reproval, the Lord then explains how he cares for wandering sheep. His words stand as a pattern for latter-day teachers in the kingdom who struggle to retain errant students like Angelique. The Lord explains that "I, even I, will both search my sheep, and seek them out" (v. 11). Searching and seeking suggest involvement beyond what is ordinarily required of the shepherd or teacher. Try to find out where Angelique is during your class. Is she sitting outside in her car? Is she in Primary with younger brothers and sisters? You have already telephoned Angelique. Try visiting Angelique at her home and asking her about interests outside of the Church. You could mail her a card with a personalized message of love and pick her up along with other class members for a fireside so you can have a chance to talk together in the car.

The Lord also explains that He "will feed them in a good pasture and upon the high mountains. . . . There shall they lie in a good fold. . . . I will cause them to lie down . . . and will bind up that which was broken, and will strengthen that which was sick" (vv. 14–16). The effort involved in a shepherd moving a flock to a good pasture suggests that he is interested in doing those things that are necessary to promote the long-term welfare of the sheep. Such should be the case with teachers of the gospel of Jesus Christ. This image suggests that Angelique deserves time, patience, and a good deal of hopefulness as efforts are made to help her return to class.

The image of the flock lying down in a good fold depicts an environment of safety and trust. Angelique will most likely return to class only after she feels safe and trusted. This may require the thoughtful involvement of other students in the class. Continue to encourage them to invite and include Angelique in personally significant ways so that she may feel the goodness of the fold.

Finally, a good shepherd is willing to bind up and strengthen the wounded and weary. Prayerfully make every effort to heal whatever breech lies in Angelique's heart.

Damaging church property or the property of others

Q: My class has experienced several instances where either personal property or Church property was damaged. On one occasion, the students were using the hymnbooks to sing a song that corresponded with our lesson. One of the students accidentally dropped a hymnbook and the binding was broken. On another occasion, one student grabbed an interesting-looking object from another student. During the ensuing tug-of-war, the object was broken. How do I handle situations like these?

A: In most cases, damage to Church property or personal property is an accident. The incident may be a result of carelessness or simply an unfortunate accident. In other cases, deliberate destruction of someone else's property may be apparent. This action may be the result of anger, hostility, or frustration. It may be helpful to explore what could be happening in the person's life to make him feel this way. Deliberate destruction of property is often a sign of poor self-esteem. Students who need to destroy the property of others are students who do not feel good about themselves. Prayerfully consider ways that you can help develop these students' feelings of self-worth.

On a more practical level, do not allow students to bring personal belongings (other than scriptures) to class unless they have permission from you to do so. Ask the students to leave any personal belongings they have brought to Church with their parents. If they do bring them to class, provide a box or a basket that they can put them in until class is dismissed.

Whenever you pass out Church property for the students to use or handle (such as scriptures or hymnbooks), explain how important it is for them to handle the property with reverence and respect before these materials are distributed. You could tell them that Church materials benefit everyone and that they need to keep them in good condition so that others will be able to use the materials after them. If there have been several incidents in your class where Church property was damaged, you could even have the children verbally commit to treating these items with care.

Accidents will still occur even after rules are made and precautions taken. If an accident is clearly unintentional, reassure the student by saying that everyone makes mistakes and encouraging the student to be more careful. If, however, a student deliberately destroys property, then that student should be held accountable. Arrangements should be made for the student to repair or replace the damaged object. These arrangements should be made privately and should only include those who are also affected by the damaged property. For example, if the item came from the meeting house library, you would want to have the student apologize to the librarian and ask what to do to set things right. Similarly, if the damage occurred to the classroom, such as a dented wall or a scratched chalkboard, you would probably need to involve a member of the bishopric. Parents should be included in the discussion since they will most likely play some kind of role in making sure damaged items are repaired or replaced. By holding students accountable for their behavior, you will be teaching them to be responsible for their own actions.

Bringing toys and other personal objects to class

Q: There are several children in my class who bring toys or other personal objects they've used in sacrament meeting into class. I constantly have to remind the children not to play with or talk about these objects during the lesson. It is becoming very disruptive. What can I do?

A: You could begin by making the children's parents aware of the problem. Ask the parents to remind their children to leave toys and other personal belongings with the parents at the end of sacrament meeting. Of course, this will not entirely eliminate the problem. Parents who have several children going to any number of different classes cannot always monitor what is in their children's pockets, so you will probably want to discuss the problem with the children in your class.

Tell the children that bringing objects that don't relate to the lesson is becoming disruptive. Ask them to leave these objects with their parents before coming to class. If, however, they forget, tell them that you will provide a box or a basket where they can put their personal belongings until class is over. Before you begin class, make sure that all personal objects are in the box. Then put the box out of reach and out of sight, perhaps in a bag or under a coat.

If it becomes apparent that the children are not putting personal objects in the box but are concealing them and bringing them out later in class, you might want to consider having two boxes. Items that go into the first box will be given to the children immediately following class, but items that have to be taken away during the lesson will go into the second box. These items will not be returned to the children until later. Make sure the children understand this plan before proceeding. It might be a good idea to make their parents aware of your plan as well.

Not bringing or using scriptures

Q: I feel that it's important for my students to use their scriptures in class. I have been trying to encourage my students to bring their scriptures to class. I have even checked to make sure that each of my students has a set of scriptures. Despite this, many of them continue to leave their scriptures at home. Even when the students do remember their scriptures, they often do not use them during the lesson. What can I do to motivate my class members to both bring and use their scriptures?

A: You are right that it is important for your students to use their scriptures in class. The scriptures have a great power to help us feel the whisperings of the Spirit. In Doctrine and Covenants 18:34–36, it says:

These words are not of men nor or man, but of me;

wherefore, you shall testify they are of me and not of man; For it is my voice which speaketh them unto you; for they are given by my Spirit unto you, and by my power you can read them one to another; and save it were by my power you could not have them; Wherefore, you can testify that you have heard my voice, and know my words.

To motivate your students to bring and use their scriptures so that they can take part in the power and influence of the scriptures, consider these words from President Ezra Taft Benson: "Always remember, there is no satisfactory substitute for the scriptures. . . . These should be your original sources" (*Teaching, No Greater Call*, 54). From President Benson's words, we come to understand that the more we use the scriptures in a prayerful and personal way, the more we will allow our students to understand the importance the scriptures can play in their lives.

You can help your students better understand the scriptures by teaching them about the study helps found within them. President Howard W. Hunter has said, "We ought to have a Church full of women and men who know the scriptures thoroughly, who cross-reference and mark them, who develop lessons and talks from the Topical Guide, and who have mastered the maps, the Bible Dictionary, and the other helps that are contained in his wonderful set of standard works" (*Teaching, No Greater Call*, 56). As we help our students understand and use the study helps in the scriptures, the scriptures will become more attainable to them.

During your lessons, try actively involving your students in the scriptures. This goes beyond merely following along as a passage is read. For example, it might be helpful-to have learners look or listen for something specific. For example, before reading a scripture passage you could say, "As we study Doctrine and Covenants 25, look for the qualities of an elect lady," or "Look for the definition of Zion as we read Doctrine and

Covenants 97:21." If you practice doing this in your own personal scripture study, you will be better able to conduct "look for" and "listen for" activities with your students.

You could also encourage your students to mark their scriptures as you teach by saying something like, "This verse contains an important principle; you may want to mark it." Your students could then shade, underline, or outline the verse or block of verses with a pencil or colored marker. Your students could also write notes in the margins of their scriptures. You could say, "I want to share a thought about this chapter. I have written it in the margin," or "Here is an excellent passage on repentance. You may want to write the word *repentance* in the margin next to it."

Finally, follow Nephi's admonition to "liken all scriptures unto us, that it might be for our profit and learning" (1 Nephi 19:23). To "liken the scriptures" means to see how scripture accounts are similar to circumstances today and to show how the principles they teach are relevant in our lives. As we help our students liken the scriptures to their lives, they will be able to see the power of the word of God in every aspect of their lives (*Teaching, No Greater Call*, 54–59).

Getting out of seat during class

Q: The students in my class have trouble staying in their seats during the lesson. One student will get up and throw something into the garbage. Another student will get up and open the door when there is a noise in the hall. Sometimes they will even get out of their seats to hand me a small piece of garbage they found on the floor. Is there anything I can do to get them to stay in their seats?

A: The first thing you can do to solve this problem is to set clear expectations regarding their behavior. Many of the children in your class may think that since they are not being noisy when they get out of their seats that they are not being disruptive. Help them to understand that getting out of their seats, even when they are quiet, distracts the other students and takes away from the lesson.

Once your expectations are clear, another thing you might try is setting boundaries that keep students from wandering around. For example, if you put the students' chairs in a circle, the only place students who get out of their chairs can go is inside the circle. This can also be done using a corner. Place your chair directly in the corner, and then set up the students' chairs in a semicircle with the walls serving as boundaries. For young children, a large blanket can serve as a boundary. Lay the blanket out on the floor when it is time for the lesson, and encourage them to remain on it until the lesson is over.

Remember that children and young people are asked to sit for a very long time when they come to church. They may need a break from time to time. When you notice them getting restless, you might want to allow some time for stretching, a brief walk outside, or an activity song from the *Children's Songbook* (try "Fun to Do," 253; "If You're Happy," 266; "I Have Two Little Hands," 272; or "Once There Was a Snowman," 249). If your classroom is large enough, you may even be able to move from place to place for different parts of your lesson. For example, you could have a story corner, a scripture table, and listening circle. When you are telling and talking about a story, you could sit in the story corner. When you are reading and marking your scriptures, you could sit at the scripture table. When you are talking and presenting information, you could sit in the listening circle, where chairs are set up in a circle.

Tipping back in chairs

Q: My class has a problem with tipping back in their chairs. One Sunday, a boy accidentally fell over when he tipped back too far. He was unhurt, but the entire class laughed so much that I had a hard time settling them back down. Since then, many of the students tip back in their chairs and actually try to tip themselves over while the other students egg them on and encourage them to topple. This has become disruptive to the lesson. What can I do?

A: The students in your class are most likely tipping back in their chairs because of the attention they receive for doing so. Randall Sprick offers the following advice, paraphrased here, on page 81 of *The Solution Book:*

Design a consequence for tipping back in the chair. A reasonable consequence for not using a chair correctly is to have the chair taken away. You could designate a spot next to you where students who have had their chairs taken away can sit. This should teach the student that having a chair is a privilege that can only be earned when treating a chair properly.

Next, discuss the problem and the consequence with your students. Allow your students to come up with reasons why tipping back in chairs is inappropriate. Some of their reasons might include the following: tipping back in chairs is dangerous because someone could get hurt; tipping back in chairs can break the chairs; when everyone tips back in their chairs, they are being disruptive to the lesson. After your students have come up with some good reasons why it is important to keep the legs of the chair on the floor, discuss the consequence with them. Tell them you will give them one warning, but on their second offense, you will take the chair away. Once they clearly understand the problem as well as the consequence, ask them to verbally commit to keeping their chairs on the floor.

When a student tips back in his chair, remind the student of his commitment and warn that the next time the commitment is broken you will take the chair away. If the student tips back in the chair a second time, take the chair away and ask the student to come sit on the floor next to you. Do not lecture or scold the student but calmly say, "It looks like you forgot how to use a chair properly, so you will have to sit next to me on the floor for the rest of class." If the student argues with you, ignore him and do not negotiate or give one more chance. In this way, you will be holding the students accountable for their actions.

If someone begins to tease the student for not having a chair, praise other students for minding their own business. Do not give attention to either the student doing the teasing or the student being punished. The next week, allow the student to sit in a chair, but remind him and the entire class of their commitment to keep their chairs on the floor and the consequence if they do not. If you are consistent with your students and refrain from giving attention to their undesirable behavior, you should find that your students will be able to sit in their chairs with all four legs touching the floor.

Asking to go to the bathroom or get a drink of water

Q: The students in my class are constantly interrupting the lesson to go to the bathroom or get a drink of water. I only allow one person to go at a time, but it seems like I always have a steady stream of kids going in and out of class. What can I do to make this less of a disruption?

A: For older children and youth, it can be effective for a problem like this to simply state an expectation and stick with it. You could begin by explaining the problem to your students. Once they understand that their frequent trips to the bathroom and drinking fountain have become disruptive, you could tell them that you expect them to go to the bathroom and get a drink of water before they come to class. Tell them that in the future they will not be allowed to leave class once they have come in. If, after you have made your expectations clear, some of your students continue to ask to leave class, say simply, "No. You know the rule. You need to take care of that before class." When the students understand that you are serious, they will probably stop asking. Class times are rarely lengthy enough to cause a problem, and if students truly need to excuse themselves, the need is usually obvious and an exception can be made.

For younger children, you might think about taking a class bathroom and water break, especially if you are teaching

Primary and the children are with you for both class time and sharing time. It would still be a good idea to encourage them to go to the bathroom or get a drink of water before class or sharing time. Then let the children know that right after class or right after sharing time, you will stop as a class to go to the bathroom and get a drink of water. If you have an especially large class, you could enlist the help of a member of the Primary presidency or one of the children's parents. If children ask to go to the bathroom during class or before sharing time, encourage them to wait until you go as a class. Of course, it is important to watch these children closely to make sure that they can wait. When the children understand that there is a plan in place, they should be willing and able to follow it.

Not behaving in the hallways

Q: What can I do to help the students in my Primary class maintain reverence in the hallway between class time and sharing time?

A: It is important not to assume that your students understand how to behave appropriately in the hallway. Many students have never been taught. The first thing you can do is to decide with your students how they should behave in the halls. You might decide that when you are in the hallways, students need to walk quietly, keep their hands and feet to themselves, talk quietly only to people near them, and stay with the class.

Once you've decided on appropriate hallway behavior, you might want to practice this behavior with your students. Take your class on a walk to see if they can behave appropriately in the halls. Tell them that the whole class will go back to the room and try again if anyone has trouble following the rules. As you practice, praise the students for following the rules. If any student violates a rule, stop the class and calmly state which rule was violated without saying who did it. Go back to the room and begin again. Continue until the entire class can behave appropriately in the halls.

When it is time to actually go to class or to sharing time, remind the students of how they are expected to behave. Any time that a student violates the rules, take the whole class back to where you started and begin again. Praise the students when they make it to class or sharing time successfully. Consistency is the key that will make the difference.

Being irreverent during sharing time

Q: My Primary students are well behaved and attentive during the lesson, but the minute we walk into sharing time, they transform into a different class. Instead of sitting quietly and paying attention, they wiggle in their seats, whisper to one another, and laugh and giggle a lot. I do my best to encourage them to be reverent, but nothing seems to be helping. What can I do?

A: Children and young people sometimes exhibit different levels of maturity in different situations. Although students behave appropriately during your lessons, they get into sharing time and for some reason, whether it is being with a larger group of kids or receiving less individual attention, they behave less maturely. This is not uncommon, but in order to deal with the situation effectively you will probably need to incorporate some slightly different methods than you use in your class.

First of all, talk with your class about the problem. Ask them to describe their own behavior during sharing time. You could say, "I've noticed that you behave differently during sharing time than you do in class. Can you tell me what some of those differences are?" When they have identified their inappropriate behavior, you could say, "I really appreciate the way you behave in class. Your reverence helps us feel the Spirit. What do you think might happen if you behaved in sharing time the way you behave in class?" They might respond that they would feel the Spirit or that the Primary presidency would feel grateful. Accept their responses and then ask, "Can I count on you to behave reverently during sharing time?" Get a verbal agreement from each one of them, and then say, "Remember, I'll be watching, and we'll follow up on this discussion next week." Following up is very important. It lets the students know that you will hold them accountable for their behavior, and your praise when they do behave well will be encouraging and motivating to them.

If your students are younger, you might also want to assign them places to sit and make this a fixed seating arrangement. You can keep talkative students away from one another, and you can seat your most disruptive students next to you or near enough that you can get their attention easily by touching them lightly on the knee, shoulder, or head. Wait until their behavior improves before you move your hand away. Even with young children you can talk to them about their behavior. Praise them when they are reverent and encourage them when you see they are trying to do better. When they understand that you expect them to be reverent, they will usually try to meet your expectations.

Something else that might help is to give your students reasons to listen. This is especially helpful if you have class following sharing time. Lead a discussion at the beginning of your class about what was talked about during sharing time. Incorporate some of the sharing time principles into your lessons. You could even sing some of the songs taught during sharing time at appropriate times during your lesson. Your students may pay better attention when they are given reasons to listen.

Chapter 4: **Solving Problems with Individual Students**

Rebecca Johnson struggled when she was a Primary teacher for the eight-year-olds in her ward. One boy in particular was extremely disruptive. Sister Johnson said of this boy, "I had never encountered a pupil like John. He would somehow disrupt my whole Primary class. . . . I am sorry to say now that I sometimes hoped he wouldn't be there on a Sunday because of his potential for disruption" ("What an Eight-Year-Old Taught Me," *Ensign*, September 1999, 20).

Often in Church classes, the majority of students are well behaved and attentive while only one or two students are disruptive. Yet these one or two disruptive students can spoil the experience for the entire class. When this occurs, it is important to work with disruptive students individually and privately to help them become self-disciplined. We'll offer a few general guidelines and then some specific suggestions. Perhaps the ideas offered here can be viewed as a foundation on which caring teachers can construct the most appropriate solution for the situation they face.

General Guidelines

It is a good idea to speak to the worst offenders in private. If a disruptive child is addressed in front of the class or with a peer, chances are the student will be more concerned with impressing others than with examining improper behavior. A power struggle could easily follow. Instead, look for a moment when the student can be talked to one-on-one, or with two adults if needed. Set specific goals together and establish a plan of action. Make this a matter of prayer, and remember the counsel in Doctrine and Covenants 121:43–44: "Reproving betimes with sharpness, when moved upon by the Holy Ghost; and then showing forth afterwards an increase of love toward him whom thou hast reproved, lest he esteem thee to be thine enemy."

One definition of sharpness is exactness. Rather than yelling and screaming and then apologizing, we may do better to clearly identify exactly what is happening and why it is not helping us teach and learn. Then we can help offending students determine specifically what they are going to do to correct the problem and commit to it. Finally, we can find times that are exactly right to praise and appreciate students as they attempt to be better.

As you meet with the student away from the attention of peers, she will usually be cooperative. If, however, the student is still belligerent, or rudely refuses to answer questions or commit to a plan, try giving her a little time alone. Being alone with the influences of the Spirit after poor behavior usually has a mellowing effect. Still, if the student remains belligerent, involve leaders and parents—not to rescue you but to help the student make a plan for change and commit to that plan

Sister Johnson, mentioned at the first of this chapter, was challenged in a teacher development lesson to improve the discipline in her class. Sister Johnson set a goal to help John, the student in her class who caused so many disruptions. That week she prayed whenever possible, hoping for the help she needed. When Sunday came around, John disrupted class even more than usual. He frequently poked or hit the child next to him. He cracked a joke with every other question asked, and he made Sister Johnson feel like she was not getting her lesson across to anyone. After class, the Holy Ghost prompted Sister Johnson to ask John to stay. The interview that followed can serve as an example for any teacher trying to help one or two disruptive children behave in a self-disciplined way:

> I pulled my chair in front of him and looked him in the eye. He looked at me for a while, then looked down at the floor.
>
> "Do you like disrupting the class and picking on the other children all that much?" I asked. He played with the hole in the knee of his jeans as he thought about it for several seconds. "It gives me something to do," he said finally.
>
> "Are my lessons that boring to you?" I asked. He answered simply, "Yes."
>
> Well, I asked for that, I thought. "Besides, my mom makes me come to Primary, and I hate it," John added.
>
> "What would you rather be doing?" "I'd rather be outside with my friends," he answered loudly and emphatically.
>
> I struggled not to react angrily. "Well, I can't help you there, but I'd like to make your stay at Primary more enjoyable. I don't want you to have to come and hate my class. Can you make any suggestions how I could help you? I could use some ideas?"
>
> As he thought for a moment, I watched the expressions on his face, feeling love and compassion for him.
>
> I could imagine him enjoying his play outside and resenting being called away as his mother made him come to Primary for reasons he did not understand.
>
> Finally, he volunteered, "You could play games with us to help us learn what you're trying to teach."
>
> "I've tried a few games. You don't seem to be interested in them," I answered. "But if I try really hard to

make the class more interesting, do you think you could try a little harder to help out and not cause trouble?"

"Yes," he said quickly, and I promised, "If you do that for me, I'll let you help me in a game next week."

He got up to leave, and as I walked him to the door I gave him a big squeeze. It seemed to embarrass him a bit. But after that day I noticed that when he would come to class, he would be the last one to leave; he stood by the door as I said good-bye to the other children, waiting for his hug.

From then on, he tried hard not to cause trouble, and I tried to show him I cared about him, involving him in activities in the classroom whenever possible. ("What an Eight-Year-Old Taught Me," *Ensign*, September 1999, 20)

Any teacher of a disruptive child can learn from Sister Johnson's experience with John. Notice that the first thing that Sister Johnson did to help John was to pray for him. She asked for help from her Heavenly Father, and He answered her prayer not only by prompting her to talk privately with John but also by helping her see John in a new light, which enabled her to feel love and compassion for him for the first time.

As this mutual feeling of love and respect grew, Sister Johnson and John were able to come up with a plan together that would improve John's behavior. Sister Johnson did not lecture to John during their private interview. Instead, she asked him questions, allowed him to make his own judgments, and even asked for his suggestions to come up with a plan that would help. After they decided on a plan, John committed to do better. Sister Johnson did not make John behave appropriately. Rather, John chose to work on changing his behavior himself with his teacher's support and encouragement. In this way, John's behavior improved through self-discipline.

As you work with disruptive students to improve their behavior, remember Sister Johnson's example. Talk privately with them and together come up with a plan for improvement.

Use questions like, "What is the problem here?" or "Do you know why I wanted to talk with you?" These questions will help them identify the inappropriate behavior on their own. You could ask them to make a value judgment about their behavior by asking questions like, "Do you think that is helping us learn the gospel?" If students respond in a rude or disrespectful way or if they just sit there silent and defensive, don't argue or let yourself get angry. Try giving them a time limit and if they still refuse to cooperate, tell them you will continue the conversation in the presence of another adult such as the ward teacher development leader or a parent.

Once students identify their misbehavior and understand the need for change, ask for their suggestions for improvement. As in the example above, these suggestions may include things they can do as well as things you can do. Create a plan from these suggestions, and then ask the student to commit to the plan. Sister Johnson asked John, "Do you think you could help out more and not cause trouble?" John committed by simply saying yes. Another way to ask for a commitment would be, "Will you shake on it?" Of course, you cannot plan the conversation in advance, and it will not follow an exact formula. Just keep in mind that your goal should be to help the student become self-disciplined, because self-discipline puts children and young people on the pathway toward discipleship.

While you are speaking with a disruptive student, don't allow yourself to become distracted by excuses. If a student says, "Well, it was Maria's fault," or "It's because my parents are getting divorced," simply say, "I understand. Nevertheless, right now we're talking about you."

Even after gaining a commitment, it is possible that the student's behavior will continue to be disruptive. Remember to be consistent and patient and to allow time for the student's behavior to improve, but if after several weeks there is still no change and the student continues to be disruptive, you may want to implement a plan that involves leaders as well as parents.

First offense: Try reminding the student of your discussion. Later in private, you could say something like, "Remember we talked about that, and you said you would try to stop. I know you can do it. Please do not behave that way again."

Second offense: Move a chair away from the other students, and have the disruptive student sit there until he shows readiness to rejoin the group. While the student is away from the other students, do not interact with him, but when he decides to rejoin the group, offer a word of encouragement. You could say something like, "I'm glad you've decided to rejoin us. Let's make this work."

Third offense: Ask a leader, such as a member of the Primary or Sunday School presidency, to take the disruptive student to another room. Perhaps the leader may need to get the student's parents to come and talk with the student until he is in control again. Then the student can return to class. Be sure to let the student know that he is loved and that you want him to be a part of the class.

Fourth offense: Invite the disruptive student's parents to come sit with him in class. Discuss the problem with the student and his parents after class. It is especially important to continue to be supportive and loving.

Do not be embarrassed or afraid to ask for help when you encounter problems. It is the responsibility of leaders to assist, support, and develop caring relationships with the teachers in their organizations. Most Church units have a teacher development leader who may also be a support, and most parents want to know about their children's behavior. They are willing to help, and together, you can make specific plans and review progress. Including the child in your conversations will show your respect for his maturity and agency (*Teaching, No Greater Call* [Salt Lake City: The Church of Jesus Christ of Latter-day Saints, 1999], 28, 86).

Specific Solutions

The apathetic student

Q: I have a girl in my class named Lucy who doesn't seem to care about anything. She sits by herself and doesn't join the class in activities. When I try to get her involved, she either shrugs or just looks at me. What can I do to help Lucy feel like a valued member of our class?

A: When a student is not showing interest in your class, the most important thing that you can do is show interest in the student. Make it a point to spend a little bit of time each week talking to the student about something that interests her. Showing the student that you care is an important step in helping her care.

An apathetic student may also benefit from responsibility. Give the student a job to do to show her that she is a necessary part of your class. Perhaps she could be in charge of taking roll or be responsible for writing responses to questions on the chalkboard or a clipboard. Outside of class, she could be asked to find an example of what is being taught or to read a story or listen to a tape that goes along with the lesson. Giving a student responsibility will show her that you trust her and that you have high expectations of her abilities.

As she carries out her responsibilities, be sure to provide her with lots of praise. Use both verbal and nonverbal forms of praise. Praise her in private as well as in front of the class. Surprise her from time to time with a note or handmade certificate of achievement.

The argumentative student

Q: I have a boy in my early-morning seminary class named Jared, who is very bright and knowledgeable about the gospel. The problem is that he is always arguing with me during the lessons. I don't mind questions that promote discussion, but he approaches subjects negatively, and this type of attitude causes the Spirit to withdraw from our class. How can I help Jared use his knowledge to promote positive class discussions that invite the Spirit into our class?

A: By discussing the problem privately with him, you can help Jared understand that arguing and other negative interactions need to be replaced with positive interactions. Jared may not even realize that his arguing is a problem. Arguing may simply be the way he has learned to communicate. Help him to understand that negative interactions, such as arguing, can drive away the Spirit while positive interactions can invite the Spirit into your discussions. Be careful not to lecture. Ask questions of Jared. Learn his opinion, and involve him in any decisions you make.

Once Jared understands the problem, come up with a plan together. For example, you could help him recognize when he is interacting positively or negatively through the use of private hand signals. Develop a hand signal that you give to Jared when he begins to argue inappropriately. Make sure that Jared understands that you expect him to stop arguing. Praise Jared whenever he interacts positively. Also praise the other students in your class when they interact positively. This will help Jared learn how to interact without arguing, and at the same time he will learn that you focus your attention on the students whose behavior deserves recognition.

Meet with Jared to discuss his progress. Ask Jared how he feels he is doing. Give him examples of times he interacted positively. Also give him examples of times he began arguing to help him understand the difference between positive and negative interactions. You could even have him come up with some ways he could have responded more appropriately. It might be a good idea to make sure he knows that you want him to bring his knowledge and experiences into your class discussions and that when he does this in a positive way, he helps bring the Spirit into the class.

Something else that might be helpful is to evaluate the

types of questions you are asking. Are you asking only "yes and no" or "factual" questions? These types of questions tend to have only one right answer and thus may easily provoke an argument. Try asking questions that prompt deeper thinking. These types of questions may give Jared an opportunity to express his thoughts. When he does, remain open to all answers. Do not try to get students to give specific answers, because they will quickly become aware of what you are doing and either stop participating or start guessing instead of thinking. Some examples of deeper-thought questions would include the following: "Why do you think this revelation came at this time during the history of Church?" "What can this story teach us today about how the Lord helps those in need?" "What if no one learned to be meek?" "How was the reaction of Laman and Lemuel different from Nephi's reaction?" "What if Laman had been more positive?" "What would have been different?"

You can also ask questions that help learners apply gospel principles in their lives: "How has this promise from the Lord been fulfilled in your life?" "How do we sometimes make the same mistake as the people in this story?" "If you were this person, what would you do?" "What are some circumstances today that are similar to the events in the scriptures?" (*Teaching, No Greater Call*, 68–69)

The bored student

Q: Brooke is always bored. When I tell the class that we're going to play a game, she rolls her eyes and says, "Games are stupid." If I ask the students to share personal experiences, she sighs and complains, "Not again." Even when she isn't making exasperating comments, she expresses her boredom by acting disgusted. How can I help Brooke become involved and enthusiastic about class?

A: Brooke's overt signs of boredom may have received plenty of attention from teachers in the past. This attention has fed her misbehavior, causing her to do it more frequently. Brooke has probably learned that when she acts bored, people will try to find out what is wrong or they will bend over backwards to find an activity that she likes. They may even try to convince her that an activity is not boring. After a while, acting bored can simply become a habit. To decrease her bored behavior and help her respond positively in class, try discussing the problem with Brooke in private. Be supportive during the discussion. Let Brooke know that you like her and accept her for who she is, but explain that if she continues to act bored all the time, she will end up offending people and coloring the mood of the whole class. You might try giving her some examples of how she responds negatively to certain situations, then asking her to suggest a response that might be better. Be sure to get Brooke's input about the problem by asking her questions like, "What about the class makes you bored?" or "What can I do to make the class more interesting for you?" You could also ask, "Why do you think acting bored might be a concern?" Come up with some ideas together. Help her understand that you will do your part to make the class interesting if she will do her part to refrain from acting bored.

Once Brooke understands the problem and has come up with some ideas for improvement, you might want to have Brooke verbally commit to change. This might be a simple yes after you have asked, "Can I count on you to do better?" Or you could ask, "Will you shake on it?" Once she has committed, tell Brooke that you are going to ignore her if she continues to act bored, but you will give her thumbs-up if she follows through with her commitment.

Meet to discuss Brooke's progress. As Brooke's behavior improves, offer her plenty of praise and encouragement. Reinforce her efforts with appropriate rewards such as a personal note of thanks. As you do this consistently, Brooke will hopefully become more involved and enthusiastic about class.

Brooke is also more likely to be enthusiastic about class when you prepare your lessons using a variety of teaching methods. Different teaching methods include audiovisual materials, brainstorming, choral readings (see page 87), object lessons, dramatizations, drawing activities, flannel boards, games, music, puppets, and reader's theater, just to name a few. Children and youth respond especially well when a variety of methods are used during the same lesson. With this variety, learners tend to understand gospel principles better and retain more (*Teaching, No Greater Call*, 89). It may also be helpful to include Brooke in helping to teach the lesson or to offer her an out-of-class challenge such as writing something to submit to the *New Era* or *Friend*. You could even have her read a Church book or listen to a tape and have her discuss her favorite parts with you.

The bossy student

Q: Lauren can be extremely bossy. I feel like this minimizes my role as the teacher, and I know that it bothers the other students when she is constantly telling them what to do. How can I help her understand that I am the one responsible for teaching the class and that the other students will be more likely to accept her when she is not bossing them around?

A: Perhaps Lauren is being bossy because she wants to feel important; you might want to begin by helping her feel important in other ways. For example, whenever you see her interacting with other students without being bossy, praise her. This will help her see that she doesn't have to boss others around to feel good. It might also help to give Lauren some sort of responsibility that she can be proud of. Perhaps she could be in charge of taking roll, writing responses to questions on the chalkboard, or organizing class devotionals. Whatever you decide on, remember that the responsibility should help Lauren feel good about herself without being bossy.

To further improve Lauren's interactions with others, you could try discussing the problem with her in private. Explain to her that being bossy will hurt the relationships she builds with others. While she may feel she is being helpful, let her know that there is a difference between being bossy and being helpful. You might ask, "Can you think of some reasons why being bossy might make others mad?" Give her some examples of the times when she has been bossy, and then ask her to give some ideas of how she could have changed her bossy behavior into helpful behavior. Do this until Lauren understands the difference between being bossy and being helpful.

Once she understands how her behavior can be more helpful, ask Lauren to verbally commit to do better. She could do this by simply saying yes after you have asked, "Can I count on you to do better?" Since bossy students tend to want to feel important, it might be a good idea to let her know that you really need her assistance to help the class be more reverent, and by refraining from being bossy, she will really help you out.

Meet to discuss progress. As Lauren's behavior improves, offer her encouragement and praise. When problems occur, continue to give her examples of her bossy behavior and ask her how she could have been more helpful. Point out times when she was helpful without being bossy. It may also help to point out that while she sees adults who seem bossy, they often act differently with those who are close to their age. She needs to be especially careful when dealing with peers or adults.

The clingy student

Q: I have a little shadow in my class named Seth. I call him my shadow because he follows me wherever I go. If I stand up to write on the chalkboard, he stands up with me and clings to my leg until I sit back down. He always pulls his chair next to mine, and he often tries to climb up on my lap. This is a problem because his constant need for attention makes it almost impossible for me to give my attention to the other students. Is there anything I can do to help Seth be more independent?

A: It might help Seth become more independent if you try ignoring his clingy attention and praising the other students in your class for being independent. When Seth sees that you give your attention to students who act independent, he may begin acting more independent himself. For example, when Seth follows you up to the chalkboard, ignore him completely and say enthusiastically to the other students, "Thank you for staying in your seats. We all learn so much better when we stay in our own seats." When Seth tries to climb up on your lap, say to the other students, "Thank you for sitting up so tall in your own seats. You are being so reverent." You could give a sticker as a reward to the other students for staying in their seats.

Be sure to give Seth plenty of praise and encouragement when he is independent. You may need to do this quite frequently at first and then gradually decrease the amount of praise you give him as he becomes more and more independent.

Of course it's hard to ignore a child hanging on your leg. Without reprimanding, you may need to physically take his arms from around your leg and hold him at a distance. Obviously, such children need attention, but when they demand it or get it by manipulating, it really doesn't fill their need. Don't hesitate to create a comfortable distance between you. You can then fill that gap by drawing closer to the child at a time of your choosing, not his. This way the attention freely given can fill the need rather than be something that is demanded or dragged out of you.

The competitive student

Q: Dominique is extremely competitive. His answers always have to be right. He always has to find the scripture first, and he always has to win the games we play. His competitiveness is creating a negative atmosphere in my class, and the other students are becoming fed up with Dominique's behavior. How can I help him?

A: It is important to understand that overcompetitive children like Dominique are often insecure with themselves. They are sometimes under the mistaken impression that they are not of worth if they are not better than everyone else. To help Dominique, you might try discussing the problem with him in private. Tell him that you are concerned that he feels like he has to be the first and the best at everything that happens in class. Ask him to come up with some reasons why this might be a concern to you. Ask him if he has noticed how negative everyone seems to feel when he acts so competitive, and see if he can come up with some ideas about how he could improve the situation. You might want to explain to him that Heavenly Father and Jesus love him whether or not he is the fastest or the best. You could tell him that Heavenly Father and Jesus are more concerned about how he treats others than about how many games he wins or questions he gets right. Let him know that he can be a real winner if he can learn to be supportive and kind to others under any circumstances.

When you feel that these concepts are clear in Dominique's mind, formulate a plan together. For example, you could come up with some private hand signals that would let Dominique know when he is acting competitively. When he sees the hand signal, he will know that his behavior needs to change. Likewise, when you are congratulating a classmate who has won a game or answered a question correctly, you could give him the thumbs-up sign as well to let him know you notice he is following through with the plan. Meet to discuss Dominique's progress. At the end of class, discuss with him how he felt he did. Offer him plenty of praise and encouragement, and reward his efforts with appropriate reinforcement such as a personal note of thanks.

It may also be helpful to limit the number of activities you plan that include competition and the number of questions you ask that require "right" answers. Try some activities in which the students must cooperate. Perhaps each could have a piece that is needed to complete a puzzle on the board, or each could have a block that is needed to build a tower together. Each puzzle piece or block could represent a concept or point in the lesson. If you wish to add an element of competition, have the class work together to race the clock or play against you rather than each other. Similarly, ask questions that encourage the students to share opinions rather than remember certain facts.

The student who hits or behaves aggressively toward others

Q: Antoine hits other students when he feels frustrated. The more I scold or show my disappointment, the more Antoine hits. How can I get this to stop?

A: Hitting is a behavior that usually occurs because the student is feeling unloved or powerless in other aspects of his life. By hitting, he feels in control, and he gets the attention he desires, even if it is negative attention. By scolding Antoine, you may actually be encouraging him to hit. Instead of focusing your attention on the student who is doing the hitting, try focusing your attention on the student being hit. You could say, "I'm so sorry that happened. Are you okay? Let's see what we can do to make sure that doesn't happen again." Then without saying a word to Antoine, move him to a seat next to you. As long as the hitting was not outrageously violent, causing tears or a bloody nose, proceed with your lesson as if nothing had happened. By ignoring the bothersome but not violent hitting, you should see the behavior diminish.

If the hitting does not decrease, however, discuss the problem with Antoine. Let him know that you understand what it is like to feel frustrated, and ask him what is making him feel frustrated. Let Antoine know that hitting is not a good way to resolve frustration, and you cannot let it continue. Implement a plan that involves your leaders and Antoine's parents.

First offense: Try giving Antoine a warning that reminds him of your discussion. You could say something like,

"Remember we talked about hitting, and you said you would try to stop. I know you can do it. Please do not hit again."

Second offense: Move a chair away from the other students, and have Antoine sit there until he shows he's ready to rejoin the group. While he is away from the other children, do not interact with him, but when he decides to rejoin the group, offer him a word of encouragement. You could say something like, "I'm glad you've decided to rejoin us. Let's make this work."

Third offense: Ask a leader, such as a member of the Primary or Sunday School presidency, to take Antoine to another room. The leader may wish to get his parents to come and talk with him until he is in control again. Then he can return to class. Be sure to let him know that he is loved and that you want him to be a part of the class.

Fourth offense: Have Antoine's parents come and sit with him in class. Discuss the problem with Antoine and his parents after class. It is especially important to continue to be supportive and loving.

Remember, do not be embarrassed or afraid to ask for help when you encounter troublesome problems. It is the responsibility of leaders to assist, support, and develop caring relationships with the teachers in their organizations. As this happens, the quality of teaching in the Church will improve. Remember that parents want to know about their children's behavior. They are willing to help, and together you can make specific plans and review progress. Including the child in your conversations will show your respect for the child's maturity and agency (*Teaching, No Greater Call*, 28, 86).

The manipulative student

Q: Anita frequently disobeys our class rules, but when I try to incorporate the consequences, she either tries to talk her way around the rule or she acts hurt and accuses me of treating her unfairly. I can't even praise the other students for good behavior because when I do, she mopes and pouts, and she mumbles that I like them better than I like her. She also tries to leave class by telling me that she has to go to the bathroom or that she has to go talk to her mom. I know that when she leaves she doesn't do either of these things, but I don't feel comfortable accusing her of lying. What can I do to make Anita feel that she doesn't have to trick me or lie to me?

A: It sounds like Anita is being manipulative. In some cases, manipulative students feel insecure. They try to control situations in order to feel important, and each time they successfully control a situation, their manipulating behavior becomes more firmly ingrained. You can help Anita begin eliminating her manipulative behavior by helping her develop a positive self-image. Praise her whenever you catch her following the rules or being honest, cheerful, and friendly. Praising her will show her that she does not have to be manipulative to get your attention or your approval. It will also help her take pride in her appropriate behaviors rather than her efforts at manipulation. You can also develop her self-image by showing interest in her. Try calling her during the week or taking interest in how she is doing at school and in other activities in which she is involved.

As you focus on building Anita's self-image, try discussing the problem privately with her. You might want to begin by asking her to identify her inappropriate behavior. You could ask, "What's the problem here?" or "Tell me what's happened?" Listen to her talk while at the same time helping her to identify her manipulative behavior. Once the behavior is identified, ask, "Is that helping us?" This will help her make her own value judgment about her behavior.

Once Anita understands that her manipulative behavior is unproductive, ask her to help you come up with some solutions to specific behaviors. For example, you could say, "Sometimes when I praise other students, you complain that I like them better than you. This isn't true. I care about you all. How could you respond differently?" Her response might be, "I could praise my classmates and be happy for them." Another example would be, "Anita, you always complain that the class rules are unfair. Do you really think the rules are unfair? What can we do about this?" Listen to her response, and then come up with a plan or compromise together. After you have talked about some specific situations and she has offered her suggestions and solutions, ask Anita to commit to improved behavior by saying, "Can I count on you to make these changes?"

Be consistent in holding her accountable for her behavior. If she doesn't follow through with her own solutions, stop for a minute and look in her direction. Let your eyes show that you are disappointed that she broke her commitment. Likewise, if she refrains from being manipulative, praise her and give her plenty of encouragement to continue. Meet with her at the end of class to encourage her to keep up the good work.

Hold your ground in dealing with manipulative students. If they try to pressure you with demands such as bringing treats, having a class party, or letting them talk during class, try using phrases like, "If I do ever bring a treat or plan a party, it will be because I want to and not because you demanded it." Or you might say, "I was called to teach you by Heavenly Father. He's the one I answer to, not you." Or you could take a slightly humorous approach: "I'm not trying to win an election or be popular. I'm trying to teach you the gospel."

The student who puts himself down

Q: I'm concerned about Zac, who is constantly putting himself down. If I ask him a question, he says that he can't answer it because he is too dumb. If I give him a compliment, such as "You look handsome today," he says, "No I don't—I'm ugly." If anything goes wrong in class, he blames himself, whether or not he had anything to do with the problem. Zac rarely says anything that does not put himself down. How can I help Zac feel better about himself?

A: It may surprise you to find out that Zac is constantly putting himself down in order to get your attention.

Zac has learned that a put-down is often followed by a compliment: "You're not dumb, Zac. You are very smart. I don't like hearing a terrific person like you putting yourself down." Zac is getting some very positive attention from putting himself down.

To help Zac stop putting himself down and at the same time improve his self-concept, try talking privately with him. This discussion should not take place immediately after a put-down, because you do not want to give him any more attention for this kind of behavior. You could ask him how he thinks missionaries or scripture heroes respond to comments or compliments. Your question might sound something like, "What do you think Nephi said to his family after they thanked him for building the ship that took them to the promised land?" Zac would probably respond that Nephi said, "You're welcome," or "You can do anything with the Lord's help." Compare these responses to the put-downs Zac usually says of himself. Tell him that you are concerned about how often you hear him put himself down and that you would like to hear him start responding like Nephi and other scripture heroes. See if you can get him to verbally commit to try. You could even have him commit by asking, "Will you shake on it?"

Once Zac has committed to eliminate put-downs, tell him that you are going to begin monitoring how often he builds himself up rather than puts himself down. Explain to him that you will ignore anything negative he says about himself and that you will praise him whenever you hear him building himself up. When you do find opportunities to praise him, it might be a good idea to tell him that he is acting more like his scripture heroes. Also look for other occurrences of good behavior, and praise him when they happen. This should teach Zac that he can get your attention when he behaves in more positive ways.

Remember to avoid any comments that would reinforce his put-downs. You could also encourage Zac to focus on others and compliment them. Poor self-image is a downward cycle.

The cycle breaker is service. Help Zac forget himself in service, whether it is a class project or a private game between the two of you, such as, "Let's see who compliments the most people sincerely right after church." You might include a private challenge to babysit while someone goes to the temple or shine his father's shoes unexpectedly.

The student with a short attention span

Q: Luca cannot seem to keep still. During class, most of my energy is spent trying to keep him in his seat. Yet even when Luca is sitting, he does not pay attention for very long. Instead, he tips back in his chair, drums his knees, looks around the room, or bothers the child sitting next to him. As a result of the frequent interruptions, my lessons seem disjointed and ineffective, and I leave class each week frustrated and tired. What can I do?

A: Luca must be easily distracted. He has probably never learned how to focus his attention, so in order to help him, you will need to teach him how to pay attention. The first thing you could try is to review some class rules with Luca privately. You could ask, "Luca, what are some of the class rules?" As he responds, help him recall and make sure he understands each rule. You could then ask him, "How do you think you're doing with following these rules?" Accept his response and then ask, "Are there any ways that you think you could do better?" He might respond, "I could stay in my seat," or "I could not talk so much." Summarize this discussion by coming up with a few clearly stated expectations. You could say, "Luca, it would really help our class if you will remember to stay in your seat, talk only when it's your turn, and not bother the other students around you. Do you think you could do those three things?" He should respond yes, and you could get him to commit even further by saying, "Let's shake on it."

The next time Luca comes to class, discreetly remind him of his commitment and of the expectations the two of you came up with. Remember that he will need plenty of feedback regarding his behavior. This feedback can be given in the form of praise and encouragement such as, "Luca you listened to that story so well. Good work!" Remember that the more severe the problem, the more frequently the student will need feedback.

There will be times when Luca forgets about or disregards the expectations set for him. When this happens, stop what you're doing and look at him. Show him with your eyes that you are disappointed in his behavior. Go on with the lesson as soon as he is behaving appropriately.

If the problem continues, move closer to him, but proceed with the lesson. Continue getting closer until his behavior improves. You may even need to put your hand on his head or his shoulder. Once his behavior improves, move back, all the time proceeding with the lesson.

Think about varying the seating arrangement so that you are not in front of the students. For example, if the chairs are placed in a circle, Luca could sit next to you. When he misbehaves, you could simply touch his knee, reminding him to sit still and listen.

Stay positive. Don't assume Luca is just out to get you. You could say for example, "I know it's hard to sit still for so long, but you've been doing so well. I know you can stay in your seat for the rest of the class."

Something else that will help Luca, as well as the other children in your class, is to make sure that your lessons are full of variety, visual aids, and engaging activities that involve things students can touch and handle. Teaching methods such as these will engage a child who has a hard time just sitting and listening. *Teaching, No Greater Call* suggests that five to seven different teaching methods be used with young children. Not so many are required for older children and youth, but students at any age benefit from a variety of teaching methods (89–90). For Luca and other students with short attention spans, break complicated tasks into small, carefully arranged steps, and break up activities into smaller units since this will enable them to better focus their attention. You might consider taking a break every now and then to stand, stretch, and get the wiggles out. By frequently shifting the kind of activities we do, we can teach within the attention span of our students.

The shy student

Q: Adam is very shy. I don't think I've ever heard him talk in my class. He has never talked to me, and when I try to talk to him, he turns his head away and won't even look at me. I'm worried that he's unhappy in class because he doesn't participate in the lessons and rarely interacts with the other students. How can I help Adam have a better experience in my class?

A: By refusing to interact with others, Adam is playing it safe. Some shy students worry about being rejected. They feel that others will not like them or will even make fun of them, so they avoid interaction. Another factor that may contribute to Adam's shyness is the attention he gets from those who encourage him to participate. There are a few things you can try to help Adam interact with you and with the other students in the class.

First, work on building his self-confidence and feelings of self-worth. Show him you care by demonstrating an honest interest in his likes and dislikes, his hobbies, and his family. To learn about these things, you may need to talk with his parents first. Then you can surprise him with a note or a homemade award for something you have learned about him. For example, if you learn that he is especially helpful with his younger brothers and sisters, give him a certificate of recognition. Be sure to make this very low key, perhaps even giving it to the student in private, because of a shy child's apprehension about being in the spotlight.

Another way that you can help build Adam's feelings of self-worth is to give him some responsibility. For example, if you put Adam in charge of taking roll each week, he could feel like he was participating in class without having to interact with anyone. As you reward him for a job well done, his confidence will grow, and he will feel the trust that you demonstrate in his abilities.

Don't try to persuade Adam to get involved. One invitation to join in a discussion or activity is enough. Once this is done, Adam must decide for himself whether or not he wants to participate. This is because coaxing gives shy students a lot of attention. Consequently, they continue to act shy because they have learned that the way to get the attention they crave is to sit back and look sad or scared. If the other students in your class try to coax Adam into participating, praise them for their efforts to get Adam involved, but tell them that Adam will participate when he is ready.

Be sure to praise Adam when he does begin to participate in class. Do not, however, direct this praise directly toward the shy child. For example, do not say, "Great job, Adam. Thank you for participating with everyone else." Remember that shy students do not like to be in the spotlight. Instead, focus your attention on all the students involved by saying something like, "That was a great discussion. Adam, Eric, and Adelle, thank you for your comments."

The talkative student

Q: Elena never stops talking. She talks to those around her. She talks to students clear across the room. She talks to people passing by in the halls, and she will even talk to me when I am right in the middle of a lesson. Nothing I try seems to help. What can I do?

A: First of all, it might help to know that you are not alone in dealing with a talkative student. Talking during class is the misbehavior that is most common and most irritating to teachers. Fortunately, it is also a behavior for which many solutions are available.

One reason that Elena may be talking so much is the attention she gets from it. When you stop what you are doing to ask Elena to be quiet, you may be giving her the attention she wants and actually encouraging her to continue talking. You can help Elena become a better listener by showing her that you give your attention to those who are behaving appropriately. To do this, try praising the students who are quiet rather than reprimanding Elena. This will focus the attention on the students who are doing what you want them to do—listening. Be sure to reinforce Elena when she begins to listen by praising her appropriate behavior.

If Elena continues talking, try using your eyes to discipline. The eyes are one of the most powerful means of communicating. A steady look directed at an offending student is often sufficient to correct misbehavior.

You can also use the power of silence. Many teachers continue to talk over a noisy class. A sudden silence—even stopping midsentence—brings a painful awareness to the violator that her actions are not going unnoticed. Do not try to talk over others. One teacher says, "I'm not just a TV or video. I don't just keep going when you're not paying attention."

Another deterrent is the power of proximity. Continue with your lesson as you move closer to the offending student. You may need to move close enough to touch the student lightly on the shoulder. This action also brings awareness that the student's actions are not going unnoticed.

Involve the uninvolved. In Elena's case, where she evidently enjoys talking, this involvement should revolve around talking. Discussions, dramatizations, choral readings, recitations, and reader's theater are all teaching methods that would allow Elena to be actively involved in the lesson through talking. Writing is also a way she could express herself without taking so much class time. Tell her you would be happy to read through her written comments and concerns if she wants to share them after class. Some teachers lightheartedly take turns with their students by saying, "Okay, I'll give you one minute to get all your talking out, and then it's my turn."

If there is still no improvement in Elena's behavior, try talking privately with her. During the discussion help her to identify her misbehavior by asking, "What do you think the problem is?" When she has identified talking as the problem, ask, "Do you think that your talking helps us learn the gospel?" This will help her make a value judgment regarding her behavior. Help her create a plan for improvement by asking, "What can you do to improve the situation?" Once she has offered some suggestions, have her commit to her plan by asking, "Can I count on you?"

The next time Elena comes to class, remind her of her commitment. Praise her when she listens or talks at appropriate times, and meet with her to discuss her progress as well as offer praise and encouragement toward continued improvement. It might be a good idea to give her examples of when she talked appropriately and to tell her how it was helpful to the lesson. You could say, for example, "Thank you for sharing that story about your mom. It really strengthened our lesson." As you do this, she will probably feel motivated to take more opportunities to talk appropriately, and your lessons will begin to benefit from her input and comments.

The unmotivated student

Q: Ivan is extremely unmotivated. I feel like I have to drag him into whatever we are doing. When I give the students instructions such as, "Please get your scriptures out," he does nothing until I coax him several times. He sighs and moves slowly and gives the distinct impression that he does not want to be in class. Is there anything I can do to get Ivan excited about learning?

A: To begin with, consider these words from President Kimball, "One cannot become a 'doer of the word' without first becoming a 'hearer.' And to become a 'hearer' is not simply to stand idly by and wait for chance bits of information; it is to seek out and study and pray and comprehend"

("How Rare a Possession—the Scriptures!" *Ensign,* September 1976, 2). Motivated students seek out, study, pray, and comprehend.

But also keep in mind this comment: "An individual's decision to study the gospel diligently is a righteous use of agency. Teachers who understand the doctrine of agency will not try to force others to learn the gospel. Instead, they will strive to teach in a way that will encourage others to put forth diligent effort to learn the gospel" (*Teaching, No Greater Call,* 208). To help you approach this goal in your teaching, the following suggestions might prove helpful:

1. A teacher's goal should be greater than just delivering a lecture about truth. Teachers should understand that the learning has to be done by the student. When a teacher takes the spotlight and does all the talking, this is almost certain to interfere with the learning of the students. A skilled teacher doesn't think, "What shall I do in class today?" but thinks, "What will my students do in class today?" A skilled teacher doesn't ask, "What will I teach today?" but "How will I help my students discover what they need to know?"

2. Nurture your own enthusiasm for studying the scriptures and the teachings of latter-day prophets. Your enthusiasm may inspire those you teach to follow your example. Always draw attention to the scriptures and the teachings of latter-day prophets as you teach and explain how and when they first became important to you. This will help students appreciate how rich and meaningful the word of God is.

3. Show students how to use the study helps in the scriptures. Teach them how to use footnotes, the Topical Guide, the Bible Dictionary, the excerpts from the Joseph Smith Translation, and the maps.

Individuals who use these study helps become more confident in their ability to use the scriptures. Instead of simply saying, "Look up the scripture," say, "I'll give you the first phrases of the scripture, and you see if you can find a key word to look up in the Topical Guide."

4. Ask questions and give assignments that require students to find answers and study the scriptures and the words of latter-day prophets. Consider ending a lesson by asking a question or giving an assignment that requires those present to search the scriptures and the teachings of latter-day prophets. Even little children can be given this type of assignment. For example, after a lesson about prayer, you could ask the children to read with their parents a scripture account or general conference talk about prayer. You may even want to have them call you when they finish the assignment.

5. Help students understand that the people in the scriptures were real people who experienced trials and joy in their efforts to serve the Lord. The scriptures come alive as we remember that the prophets and other people in the scriptures experienced many of the same things we do.

6. Show learners how to find answers to life's challenges in the scriptures and in the teachings of latter-day prophets. Openly encourage them to study the scriptures and teachings. For example, you could help them use the index in the conference issue of the *Ensign* or Topical Guide in the scriptures to search for counsel on topics such as comfort, forgiveness, prayer, repentance, or revelation. What topics are of most interest to the unmotivated student?

7. Bear your testimony to your students of the Savior as the center of all that the scriptures and latter-day

prophets teach. As those you teach see the Savior in the scriptures and in the teachings of latter-day prophets, their hunger to study will increase and their testimonies will be strengthened (adapted from *Teaching, No Greater Call* , 61–62).

If more motivation is needed, you may look for ways to provide an audience for the student. Could what is being learned or studied be shared in a class of younger students? Could the student be expected to give a talk or help teach the lesson? Just as you as a teacher are motivated to study and prepare because you are presenting your lesson to others, unmotivated students often perk up when they are put in a teaching or presenting role.

The complainer

Q: Rachel is constantly complaining. No matter what we do, Rachel can always find something about it that she doesn't like. The story is too long. The songs are too high. The room is too hot, or the scriptures don't make any sense. Is there anything I can do to stop the complaints?

A: Complaining, like many behaviors, usually continues because it gets reinforced. Rachel has probably received attention for her complaints in the past. Perhaps you've heard yourself say, "Rachel, you have a beautiful voice. I know you can hit the high notes." Even a rebuke, such as, "I know it's hot in here, but there is nothing we can do about it," gives Rachel the attention she desires.

To help Rachel stop complaining, try discussing the problem privately with her. Be sure that the discussion does not take place immediately following a complaint, so that the attention does not reinforce the behavior. You might begin the discussion by asking Rachel why she complains so much. Be ready: her answer may very well be in the form of a complaint. But accept the complaint and then ask, "Do your complaints help the class learn?" She will probably say no. But even if she doesn't, help her to understand that not only are her complaints disruptive to the class, but they can also eventually cause problems with the people she associates with. You could remind her that the pioneers had plenty to complain about, but their complaints did not make the journey any easier.

Once you have helped her to understand the problem, ask, "Can you think of something we can do that will help?" Together come up with some solutions. You could praise her for her positive responses in order to teach her how to respond appropriately. At the same time, when she does complain, you could look at her and show her with your eyes that you expect the complaining to stop. Once you've come up with a solution, get her to verbally commit to what you have decided. You could even ask something like, "Will you shake on it?"

Meet with Rachel to discuss her progress. Provide Rachel with plenty of encouragement as she progresses. You could give her examples of some of her complaints and ask her how she could have responded differently. Praise her for coming up with appropriate suggestions.

Something else that might help would be to finish each class by having all the class members tell their favorite part of the lesson or one of the things they love most about the Church. Hearing positive comments from those around her and being given opportunities to make positive remarks herself should help Rachel learn how to respond more appropriately.

The daydreamer

Q: Skyler never seems to be paying attention. He is not disruptive. On the contrary, he is the quietest boy in my class, but I'm sure that he is not learning anything. He looks out the window or up at the ceiling. He stares at the floor or straight ahead, but he always has a faraway look in his eyes. Whenever I try to draw him into the lesson by asking questions or involving him in an activity, he always asks for me to repeat my questions or instructions. Is there anything I can do to help Skyler become an engaged member of our class?

A: You are right to be concerned about Skyler. Many teachers would not see Skyler's behavior as a problem since he is not being disruptive. Yet learning how to pay attention is an important part of becoming self-disciplined. To help Skyler become more engaged in the learning experiences of your class, try discussing the problem privately with him. Tell Skyler how much you enjoy having him in class and how much you appreciate the fact that he never disrupts class. Explain to him, however, that you are concerned because there are many times that he does not pay attention. Ask him if he sees how this can be a problem. It may help to ask how he would feel if he met the prophet or what he would ask him. Ask, "How would you show respect to the prophet if you were in an interview with him or if he were teaching you in a small group?" His answers could then be related to the problem of his inattention in class. Using these answers as a guide, help him see that there is more to reverence than just sitting quietly. Help him to understand that being reverent means listening to the lesson and learning about Jesus in order to follow His example and become like Him. Ask Skyler if this sounds important to him, and ask him what he thinks he could do in class to become more like Jesus. Help him set the goal to begin paying attention in class in order to accomplish this important goal. Ask him to commit to what you have discussed by asking, "Can I count on you to pay better attention?" or "Is that a promise?"

Before each lesson, discreetly remind Skyler of his commitment to pay attention. When he is engaged in learning with the rest of the class, be sure to praise him and offer him plenty of encouragement. When you notice that he is daydreaming, you might simply wait quietly for a moment or say his name to get his attention. Then show him with your eyes that he needs to stop daydreaming.

Meet to discuss Skyler's progress. During these meetings, praise Skyler for his efforts and encourage him to keep trying. Be sure to point out times when you have noticed him engaging in learning, and have him report on times when he was daydreaming. Have him develop ideas that will help him pay better attention. If he suggests playing more games in class or seeing a segment of a Church video or telling more stories, honor these requests and incorporate them into your lesson.

The teacher's resource guide *Teaching, No Greater Call*, suggests the following teaching methods you could try in your lessons to help Skyler engage in learning:

Choral Readings—A group reads scripture passages, poetry, or prose together. This method could be used to present scripture accounts, stories, poems, and other information. Be sure to select materials that support the lesson topic. These materials may be found in the scriptures, Church-produced magazines, Church-produced manuals, and the *Children's Songbook* or Church hymnbook.

Dramatizations—Those you teach can gain a greater understanding of the gospel by dramatizing accounts from the scriptures, Church history, or Church magazines. Dramatizations should relate clearly to the lesson, should help learners remember gospel principles, and should not distract from the sacredness of scriptural or historical events. Be sure to leave enough time in the lesson to ask participants what they learned. Help them relate the message of the dramatization to their own lives.

Drawing Activities—Learners can better understand gospel principles when they draw pictures. Drawing allows them to explore and express understanding and feelings of gospel stories and principles being discussed. Students could draw their own individual pictures, or they could make a class mural. They could each draw a part of a story and then put the drawings together. Students could also make drawings that express how they feel about stories, lessons, or songs. With older students, a

Pictionary-type activity may be engaging.

Visuals—Students learn through all their senses. Sometimes, teachers tend to rely heavily on the spoken word, but teachers who desire to increase their students' ability to understand and learn will also use visuals. Most students will learn better and remember longer when you present ideas using pictures, maps, word groupings, or other visuals rather than merely speaking. (163–166, 182)

The loner or the student who feels left out

Q: Malik doesn't seem to have any friends. I've talked to some of the more mature students in my class and asked them to befriend Malik, but he seems to reject their efforts. I've seen some of the sincere efforts they have made, but Malik continues to complain to me about how no one likes him. I'm confident that the other students would be his friends if he would let them. Is there anything I can do to help Malik accept their efforts at friendship?

A: There are perhaps a few reasons that Malik is unable to make friends. The first may be that he has developed a poor self-image. If he does not think much of himself, he cannot imagine how anyone else could like him. The most important thing that you can do for Malik is to help him develop a more positive self-image. You can do this by showing genuine interest in him. Find out what he is interested in and talk to him about these interests. Talk to his parents and ask them to let you know about significant events in Malik's life, so you can give him praise and encouragement. Help him see what a great person he is so that he will feel as though he is someone worth liking.

Another reason that Malik is unable to make friends may be that he has learned that he can get attention and sympathy from teachers when he tells them the other students are mistreating him. To remedy this, it is important for you to begin responding neutrally any time Malik tries to gain your sympathy. A neutral statement would be something like, "That's too bad." Once you have said "That's too bad," continue with what you were doing. Do not sympathize with him, and do not try to find out if what he said about the other students is true. It is especially important not to criticize the other students in front of Malik. If you do these things, Malik may learn that he will not get attention for feeling sorry for himself.

It is important for you to talk with Malik about the problem, especially since you have already asked the other students to try to befriend him. Pay close attention to how the other students interact with him so that you can help Malik see how the other students are trying to help. You could ask him, "How did it make you feel when Desmond invited you to sit next to him?" or "I noticed that Jasmine shared her scriptures with you today. What did you think of that?" It might also be helpful to show Malik that he can initiate positive interactions. For example, remind Malik that just as it makes him feel good when someone says hi to him or asks him how his day is going, he can make someone else's day by giving a cheerful hello. As you help Malik recognize the other students' efforts at friendship and teach him how to return that friendship, you should begin to see an improvement in his self-image.

It might also be helpful to get Malik involved in serving others. He could help with some of the younger students during sharing time, or he could share a talent at a Cub Scout den meeting or during an activity day event. You could even find ways that Malik could serve the other students in your class. Remember that "we grow to love people as we serve them. When we set aside our own interests for the good of another in the pattern set by the Savior, we become more receptive to the Spirit" (*Teaching, No Greater Call*, 12).

The teaser/practical joker

Q: Paul is always teasing or playing practical jokes on the other students. I know that his behavior makes the others angry because they constantly tell me about the things Paul does and ask me to get him to stop. Between Paul's practical jokes and the others' tattling, I simply cannot teach an effective lesson. What can I do?

A: The goal of the teaser and practical joker is to get attention. The teacher gives him attention by scolding and rebuking him, and the other students give him attention by becoming angry with his actions. For this type of student, anger can be a highly reinforcing reaction. When he is "told on," he obtains attention from both teacher and student at the same time, and an investigation of who did what will sometimes follow. The teaser or practical joker continues to misbehave because he is reinforced by all of these various responses.

To improve conditions in your class, you could start by getting the entire class involved. The other students should learn to ignore Paul's actions. Help them understand that ignoring inappropriate behavior makes it less likely that the behavior will happen again (see "Attention getting," page 18 in this book). Once this principle is understood, you might try creating a rule about respecting one another. You could ask the class why they think it is important that all students have the right to be respected. Their responses may include some or all of the following: "When students feel respected, they are free to learn and grow and participate in class without fear of rejection or ridicule." Once the students have responded, have them help you make a list of things other class members can do to make sure everyone feels respected. Make sure the list includes "No Teasing" and "No Practical Joking."

Once you have established a rule, talk privately with Paul about the rule. Ask him, "Paul, what do you think you could do to show more respect to the other members of our class?" Help him identify his teasing and practical joking as an area needing improvement. Ask him, "Do you think your teasing helps you or any of the other students learn about the gospel?" If he doesn't say no, then say, "Take a minute and think about it." When he finally admits it doesn't help, then you can ask, "What can you do about it?" Help him come up with some solutions, and then encourage him to commit verbally by asking, "Is that a promise?" At the end of your discussion, you will have helped Paul identify his own inappropriate behavior, make a value judgment regarding that behavior, create a plan for improvement, and commit to the plan.

The next time Paul comes to class, remind him of his plan and commitment. As you observe Paul interacting positively with the other students in you class, offer him praise and encourage him to continue. If, however, he begins to tease the other students, stop what you are doing, look directly at him, and show him with your eyes that you are disappointed with his behavior. You could also move closer to him as you continue with your lesson. As you get closer to him in proximity, he should realize that you are aware of his behavior and expect him to stop.

Meet with Paul to discuss his behavior. Praise him as he improves, and point out times when you heard him teasing. Ask him how he could have improved his behavior in these situations. Be sure to be consistent in following up on your expectations.

Students with intellectual impairments

Q: I was just called to serve as a Sunday School teacher in a class that includes a boy with mental impairments. What can I do to make class a good experience for him and, at the same time, teach him and the other children in my class about the gospel of Jesus Christ?

A: First of all, it might be helpful to understand a little more about intellectual impairments. According to Elizabeth VanDenBerghe:

> Children with intellectual impairments usually do not have a disease, suffer from mental illness, or remain eternal children. Rather, they grow mentally,

and sometimes physically, at a slower-than-average rate. They can and do learn communicative, social, academic, and vocational skills. It may take them longer to learn, depending on whether the level of retardation is mild, moderate, severe, or profound. ("Helping and Being Helped by the Intellectually Impaired," *Ensign*, October 1993, 28)

Sister VanDenBerghe further explains that different factors cause mental retardation. Genetic irregularities account for a variety of conditions, the most common of which is Down Syndrome. Most causes of retardation, however, are nongenetic, caused by problems during pregnancy, complications at birth, brain injuries, seizures, exposure to toxic chemicals, deprivation, and accidents. Because causes for intellectual impairment are numerous and degrees of retardation vary greatly, some individuals will require more help than others.

Sister VanDenBerghe suggests that for a teacher of an intellectually impaired child, overcoming personal fears and prejudices may be the most important service. She explains that "only after taking that step can friendship and assistance begin" ("Helping and Being Helped by the Intellectually Impaired," 31). Sister VanDenBerghe relates an instance where Cheryl Knaub, the mother of two sons with mild intellectual impairments expressed appreciation for the gesture her bishopric made in having an expert speak to the ward in sacrament meeting. She observes, "Education is the only way for people to understand the range of mental disabilities that exist" (31).

It is also important to remember that children with intellectual impairments want and need to be treated like others. Judy Hales, mother of an intellectually impaired son named David, appreciates it when teachers and leaders expect the same standard of behavior from him as from any other child. She says, "I think it's wonderful that his Primary teachers will come to me and ask, 'What's the best way to discipline David?' rather than overcompensate for him. It really helps him progress" (32).

Another mother sometimes feels like asking her well-meaning friends who indulge her son's misbehaviors, "Would you want to encourage your child to do that? Believe me, it will only hurt my son in the long run to reinforce bad habits" (32).

With these ideas in mind, Sister VanDenBerghe offers some suggestions for teaching the gospel to students with intellectual impairments.

Be sincere:

These students know if you're a phony or if you're a true representative of Christ's love for them. It's also important to consult with parents. Find out about the child's interests as well as abilities and limitations. Ask if you should be aware of any medications the child is taking. Ask about the most effective and appropriate ways to encourage good behavior.

Adapt regular classes to the individual:

Children and youth with intellectual impairments all need to be with their peers as much as their peers need to be with them. A teacher's aide, preferably not the parent or guardian of the individual with the disability, could provide diversions when needed. A box of gospel-centered toys or activities, or the assignment of special responsibilities (such as returning something to the meetinghouse library) can provide a break. Focus on the positive, and compliment even the smallest efforts. Prepare the student ahead of time to answer a question. Find out a talent, any talent, and have the child use it. This will facilitate active involvement and enable you to make sure the student enjoys an environment that allows interaction.

While teaching, be sure to use concrete examples:

People with mental disabilities have difficulty grasping abstract ideas. For many, the best visual aid is the real thing, such as an actual iron rod. The second best is a model. The third best is a picture. Slow down the pace. Divide up the lesson to teach one concept at a time, and then repeat the concept several times. People with intellectual impairments often have a short memory and learn best by repetition. Most teachers find such clear teaching can benefit all children in the class.

Foster peer acceptance:

Tell the class about the student and discuss the nature of the disability. Try using a "buddy system" where different students are assigned to walk a fellow student with a mental impairment to class, help during games, or even call during the week. Show love through consistency, and treat the student like you would want your own family member treated.

Students with physical impairments

Q: In our ward, we have a young man who is blind and a Primary-aged child who is in a wheelchair. Although neither of these children is in my class, I would like my students to learn to love and appreciate them. Do you have any suggestions?

A: The fact that you are interested in having your students become better acquainted with these children with physical impairments shows that you are on the right track. Children and young people with physical impairments are no different intellectually than others, yet their disabilities sometimes cause those around them to question and be uncomfortable. The most important thing you can do for your students is to teach them to love, understand, and accept those with physical impairments. President James E. Faust asks this question:

Is it not possible to look beyond the canes, the wheel-
chairs, the braces, and the crutches into the hearts of
the people who have need of these aids? They are human
beings and want only to be treated as ordinary people.
They may appear different, move awkwardly, and speak
haltingly, but they have the same feelings. They laugh,
they cry, they know discouragement and hope. They do
not want to be shunned. They want to be loved for what
they are inside, without any prejudice for their impairment. Can there not be more tolerance for differences?
("The Works of God," *Ensign*, November 1984, 59)

The need for more tolerance is evidenced in the experience of a young man with cerebral palsy. His physical condition often drew unkind remarks or misunderstandings. Others
unintentionally showed rejection and discomfort around him
because of their lack of information. He observed that it usually took his roommates an entire semester to realize that there
was a sound mind in his body (Gary Bunker, "Mocking Our
Brother," *Ensign*, April 1975, 40).

Just like this young man, others have overcome physical
challenges to lead more than productive lives. Helen Keller
conquered not one but three physical handicaps. She became
blind, deaf, and mute before she was two years old. Yet she
learned to read, write, and speak. President Thomas S. Monson
teaches that history is full of examples of people with physical
handicaps who went on to greatness. The Greek poet Homer,
the English poet John Milton, and the American historian Wil-
liam Prescott were all blind. Athenian Demosthenes, greatest
of all orators, had weak lungs and a hoarse voice, and he stut-
tered. And the German composer Ludwig van Beethoven continued to compose even after he became totally deaf.

Hundreds of others who are not so famous have also overcome insurmountable odds to achieve success. You will do
your students a great service if you show respect for persons
with disabilities and help the students understand that those
with physical impairments can rise above their impediments

to accomplish the mission Heavenly Father needs them to perform here on earth. To do this, Pat Graham offers the following ideas:

First, teach your students that when Jesus lived upon the earth, people with disabilities or diseases were often treated unkindly. People were afraid of them and forced them to live apart from their families and friends. But Jesus taught us to love others and to treat them the way that we would want to be treated if we had similar problems.

Next, explain to your students that doctors today can help many injured or diseased parts of our bodies to heal, but sometimes parts of our bodies cannot be made to work right. Some eyes cannot see. Some ears cannot hear. And some legs do not walk. Those with disabilities need our loving understanding. Jesus was kind to those who were not physically well. He healed those who were lepers, invalids, blind, and lame. We can be like Jesus and help others feel better by treating them kindly and helping them learn and grow despite their physical limitations.

Once you have taught these principles to your class, you could plan some experiences to help teach empathy. Perhaps these could be done as part of an activity day or fireside so as not to distract from your lessons.

Have your students learn some sign language, then try to communicate using only signs. Blindfold some children and have others act as their guides. Try to obtain a Braille book and have children write the alphabet, their initials, or their names in Braille. You could put socks over several children's hands and have them try to button their shirts or tie their shoes. Have them take a walk through the church building and point out all the places that are or are not accessible to a wheelchair. Help them experience the frustration of dyslexia by trying to write words while looking at the reflection of a pencil in a mirror.

After the students in your class have gone through some of these experiences, emphasize to them that these activities represent only some of the problems faced by people with physical limitations. Once they have gained a better understanding of what it would be like to have physical impairments, highlight one of the disabled children in your ward. Involve the child's parents, and discuss things like what the child has accomplished, his likes and dislikes, his goals and plans for the future, his hobbies and friends, and so on. By doing these things, you will help your students begin to see that children and youth with physical impairments are very much the same as other children and youth ("Sharing Time: Being Kind, Like Jesus," *Friend,* April 1987, 26, 34).

Index

About the Authors

Katie Van Dyke graduated with honors from Brigham Young University with bachelor's and master's degrees. She is a gifted writer and an exceptional editor. Katie maintains a deeply rooted love for education and finds great joy in the art of teaching well. As a full-time homemaker, she has organized and administered grassroots educational pursuits that have greatly benefited children in the communities in which she has lived. Her ongoing advocacy of thoughtful education makes her an invaluable resource from which professional and lay teachers have drawn encouragement through seminars and in-service training presentations.

Most important, Katie is the mother of seven children. Conveying a love for literacy and meaningful educational pursuits to her children constitutes a core family value in her work as a mother.

Katie's has served as Primary president, Relief Society instructor, and Cub Scout leader. Her favorite calling in the Church has been ward nursery leader. She and her husband, Blair, live in Cedar Hills, Utah.

Brad Wilcox, who earned a Ph.D. at the University of Wyoming, is an associate professor of education at Brigham Young University. A popular author and speaker, he frequently speaks at Especially for Youth programs and BYU Education Week.

Brad has published several tapes and books, including *Pornography: Satan's Counterfeit; Filling Your Testimony Tank; Tips for Tackling Teenage Troubles; Growing Up: Gospel Answers about Maturation and Sex;* and *Big Ideas for Little Budgets,* cowritten with John Bytheway.

Brad has served in a variety of Church callings, including bishop. From 2003 to 2006, he served as president of the Chile Santiago East Mission. He and his wife, Debi, are the parents of four children.

0 26575 79185 3